The
Secret of Jewish Femininity

The
Secret of Jewish Femininity

Insights into the Practice of
Taharat HaMishpachah

Written by

Tehilla Abramov
and
Malka Touger

Based on
Tehilla Abramov's Hebrew manual for her
Taharat HaMishpachah teacher's training course

Targum/Feldheim

First Published 1988
ISBN 0-944070-04-3

Copyright © 1988 by Tehilla Abramov and Targum Press

Edited by Howard Shapiro

Phototypeset at Targum Press

Published by:
Targum Press Inc.
22700 W. Eleven Mile Rd.
Southfield, Mich. 48034

Distributed by:
Philipp Feldheim Inc.
200 Airport Executive Park
Spring Valley, N.Y. 10977

Distributed in Israel by:
Nof Books Ltd.
POB 23646
Jerusalem 91235

Printed in Israel

הספר נכתב בהתייעצות עם מרן הגאון
הרב שלמה זלמן אויערבאך זצ"ל
ובהתייעצות בדברים מסוימים עם מרן הגאון
הרב יוסף שלום אלישיב שליט"א

הספר כולו היה למראה עיני מרן הגאון
הרב שלמה זלמן אויערבאך זצ"ל
והסכים לכל ההלכות שבספר

מתוך עמוד של כתב־היד של הספר עם הערות בכי״ק של מרן הגרש״ז אויערבאך זצ״ל

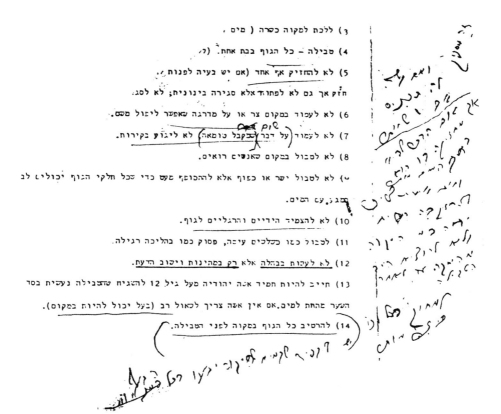

3) ללכת למקוה כשרה (מים .

4) טבילה – כל הגוף בבת אחת. (ו'

5) לא להחזיק אף אחד (אם יש בעיה לפנות

חזק אך גם לא לפתוח אלא סגירה בינונית; לא לסג.

6) לא לעמוד במקום צר או על מדרגה שאפשר ליפול משם.

7) לא לעמוד (על דבר שמקבל טומאה) לא ליגוע בקירות.

8) לא לטבול במקום שאנשים רואים.

ט) לא לטבול ישר או כפוף אלא להתכופף שם כדי שכל חלקי הגוף יכוליו לב

תבג. עם המים.

10) לא להצמיד הידיים והרגליים לגוף.

11) לטבול כמו כשהלכים עיזה, פסוק כמו בהליכה רגילה.

12) לא לעכות בבהלה אלא רק בסתינות ויכוב הדעת.

13) חייב להיות חסיד אבה יהודיה מעל גיל 12 להשגיח שהטבילה נעשית בסד

הער שהחת למים.אם אבה אשה צריך לכאול רב (בעל יכול להיות במקום).

14) להרסיב כל הגוף במקוה לפני הטבילה.

Letter of Endorsement from
HaGaon HaRav Shmuel Auerbach, *shlita*
the son of Maran HaGaon HaRav Shlomo Zalman Auerbach. zt"l
and HaGaon HaRav Yosef Sholom Elyashiv, *shlita*

BS"D   6 Nissan 5756

I hereby acknowledge and express admiration for the lofty deeds, in the foundation of *kedushas Yisrael*, of a man of great spirit, HaRav Yirmiyohu Abramov, *shlita*, and his wife, Tehilla, *shetichyeh*, who, for over twenty-five years, have brought to the public the Torah of the Jewish home and *taharas hamishpachah*. All that they do and have done has been in consultation and under the guidance of my master, my father, my teacher, my rebbe Gaon Yisrael. *zt"l*. They also established the organization Jewish Marriage Education (JME) with his encouragement. All the material they teach in the teacher's training course on the subject of the Jewish home received the *haskamah* (approbation) and *berachah* (blessing) of my master, my father, my teacher, my rebbe, Gaon Yisrael, *zt"l*, in consultation with Maran HaGaon HaRav Yosef Sholom Elyashiv, *shlita*, may he be distinguished for a long and good life. These do not need, *chas v'shalom* (God forbid), a *haskamah*. I come only to testify and acknowledge that which has already been established.

Their lot is fortunate in this world and in the next, and may Hashem continue to give them the strength to disseminate the word of Hashem — the *halachos* of *kedushas Yisrael* — and we should speedily, in our day, merit that the world fill with knowledge of Hashem... amen. May it be his will.

With all expressions of blessing,
Shmuel, the son of my master, my father, my teacher,
my rebbe, Gaon Yisrael, Shlomo Zalman Auerbach, *zt"l*

"I am in accord with the words written here."
Yosef Sholom Elyashiv

ד' אדר"ש תשד"מ

אל קהילות קודש, אחינו ואחיותינו
אשר ביהנוסבורג דרום אפריקה ד' עליהם יחיו

שלום וכל טוב סלה,

ידוע לכל ערך שמירת מצות טהרת המשפחה, שלמענה מסרו
אבותינו ואמותינו את נפשם לקיימה בשעתה ולהנחילה לדורות
הבאים אחריהם עד עולם, תמיד ידעו כי משפחה יהודית היא טבעת
זהב בשרשרת הדורות.

לצערנו הרב התרופפה מצוה זו באחרונה, והיא טעונה חיזוק
ועידוד מרובה, ללמדה ולהסבירה.

והואיל וכעת נמצאת אצלכם העסקנית הדגולה **תהילה אברמוב**
תחי', אחת הנשים החשובות והיא אחת העסקניות שלנו העוסקה
מטעמנו בהדרכה ולימוד הלכות שמירת המצוה לכן ביקשנו ממנה
לנצל את שהותה בדרום אפריקה ליסד ולכונן שם ארגון נשים
שמתפקידו יהיה לחזק את ענין שמירת טהרת המשפחה ולהרבות
מספרם של בתים ומשפחות אשר יהיו בתים שישמרו בהם על טהרת
המשפחה ועל קדושת ביתם.

ארגון זה יהיה מסונף כסניף שלנו בדרום אפריקה הן בהדרכה
והכוונה ואספקת חומר הסברה, חומר לימודי ועיוני וכו'.

נדמה כי מיותר להרבות דברים בנידון, כי כל איש ואשה האמונים
לעם ישראל ולתורתו לערוך נאמנה גודל הזכות של כל מי אשר יתן יד
למען מטרה גדולה ונשגבה זו.

והשי"ת יזכה אתכם שתהיו ממזכי הרבים להרבות משפחות
בישראל אשר יהיו משכן להשכינה הקדושה ולדורות ישרים מבורכים.
ואנו ברכה כי חסד השם יהיה עליכם להשכיל ולהצליח לרומם קרן
טהרת ישראל וליזכות עם כל בית ישראל לחזות מהרה באור פני מלך
משיח צדקנו אמן.

בכל הכבוד והברכה מעיר הקודש תובב"א
יהושע לוי

המרכז הארצי למען טהרת המשפחה בישראל/ירושלים

אך למחסור להוסיף דברים על כל האמור, אשרי האיש אשר
יהיה נמנה לדבר מצוה גדולה שהיא יסוד היסודות לקיום בית
ישראל בצביונו הטהור והמקודש, ולהגדיל טהרה ולהאדירה
להקמת דורות כשרים נאמנים להשי"ת לתורתו ומצוותיו

הכו"ח למען המצוה

הרב שלמה זלמן אויערבוך	**הרב שלום משאש**
נשיא המרכז לטהרת המשפחה	הרב הראשי ירושלים
ירושלים	

Rabbi CHAIM P. SCHEINBERG
KIRYAT MATTERSDORF
PANIM MEIROT 2
JERUSALEM, ISRAEL

הרב חיים פנחס שיינברג
ראש ישיבת "תורה אור"
וכורה הוראה דקרית מטרסדורף
ירושלים טל. 5319151

Although I have not reviewed the *halochos* in this work, I deem it a privilege to write this letter of approbation for the idea behind it.

The survival of the Jewish people as a holy nation has always depended on the determination of its married women to live up to the Torah standards of *Taharat HaMishpachah* despite every obstacle. Legion are the tales of heroism displayed by daughters of Israel who braved the threats of enemies and dangers of climate to fulfill this special mitzvah which endowed their families with purity and sanctity.

In our own time the physical obstacles are, thank God, no longer any impediment to a woman's ability to observe all the laws of family purity. The danger today is one of ignorance of the laws of *Taharat HaMishpachah* and the importance of observing them.

This is why it is such a pleasure to welcome the publication of an excellent work which presents both the laws and the significance of *Taharat HaMishpachah* in a style and language which so many of our generation so desperately require in order to become more familiar with a treasure which might otherwise remain beyond their reach. It is fitting that this work, the fruit of years of effort which Mrs. Tehilla Abramov has invested in promoting *Taharat HaMishpachah*, will, with God's help, be extended to the entire English-speaking world through the efforts of the Central Committee for *Taharat HaMishpachah*.

It is my *brocho* that *Hashem* bless with even greater success the historic efforts of all who disseminate the learning of *Taharat HaMishpachah* to our people and that Heaven open the eyes of all the daughters of Israel throughout the world to the treasure of personal and family happiness which awaits them when they live by the ideas presented in this work.

Chaim Pinchus Scheinberg

Rabbi Chaim Pinchus Scheinberg
Tishrei 5748

RABBI S. WASSERMAN
PONIM MEIROT 15/10
MATERSDORF, JERUSALEM
ISRAEL (02) 537-420

הרב שמחה וסרמן
רח' פנים מאירות 15/10
מטרסדורף - ירושלים

"...And it shall come to pass that when all of these things which I have placed before you...the blessings and the curses...you will call them to mind...and you will return completely to Hashem...Hashem *will also return to look after your exiles...and will have compassion on you....*"

(Devorim *30:1-3)*

    Our generation has witnessed the outpouring of the Divine wrath that caused unparalleled destruction and tragedy to our people. Now we are shown how the *hashgachah* rebuilds the Jewish nation by imbuing an ever-growing thirst for Torah and by inspiring the establishment of the happy and meaningful Jewish home. The *hashgachah*, at the same time, grants us its emissaries to inspire the Jewish woman in her role as mother of a pure and holy generation, deserving to welcome *Mashiach* and our redemption.

    I am grateful for the privilege of adding a note to this work which calls for the purity and holiness of the Jewish future.

Rabbi Simcha Wasserman
Tishrei 5748

הרב ישראל גנס

רח׳ פנים מאירות 2

קרית מטרסדורף, ירושלים 473 94

טלפון 531782

בס״ד ....

I have seen the book, *The Secret of Jewish Femininity,* written by Mrs. Tehilla Abramov, and I have checked the *halachot* in it.

I have found the book to be worthy of publication as it will be of great benefit to all Jewish women by furthering the Purity of *Am Yisrael.*

In the merit of this great mitzvah of *Taharat HaMishpachah,* may *HaKadosh Baruch Hu* shed over us a spirit of purity from above and may we merit the final redemption speedily in our time. Amen.

Yisrael Ganz
Tishrei 5748

OHR SOMAYACH אור שמח

"Dor, dor vedorshou"

Each generation, say our Talmudic Sages, has its own special needs, its own unique form of communication and its own Heaven-sent individuals to effectively communicate the answers to its needs.

In an age when the sacred institution of marriage is so threatened by the excesses of a permissive and self-centered society, many Jews have begun to look to the time honored practice of Family Purity as an anchor for the preservation of their personal identity and their marital happiness.

Rather than looming as a final destination on the road of commitment to a Torah life style, Family Purity has emerged as a major catalyst in convincing the newcomer of the tangible benefits of living in harmony with the prescription offered by the divine Creator of man and woman.

This exciting potential of courses in Jewish Marriage Education was discovered by Mrs. Tehilla Abramov, wife of Ohr Somayach Educational Director, Rabbi Yirmiyohu Abramov, while assisting her husband a few years ago during his tour of duty as the head of Ohr Somayach operations in the Jewish community of South Africa. The scores of families who went from these courses on Jewish Marriage to a fuller experiencing of a Torah life inspired her to extend these efforts upon returning to Israel. In addition to her work with The Central Committee for *Taharat HaMishpachah* as a trainer of Family Purity counsellors, she also gives a course for the wives of the participants in the Ohr Somayach Teachers Training Program committed to assisting their husbands in communicating Jewish values throughout the world.

This book is both the echo of the historic work which Mrs. Abramov and her colleagues have done on several continents and a harbinger of the dramatic impact which education in Family Purity is certain to have on an entire generation anxious to discover the wisdom and beauty of a Torah-guided family life, and to strengthen themselves in the observance of its requirements.

The entire Jewish community salutes the Central Committee for *Taharat HaMishpachah* and Mrs. Abramov upon this publication of a truly effective response to the most sensitive need of our generation.

Rabbi Mendel Weinbach
Dean
Ohr Somayach Institutions

המרכז הארצי למען טהרת המשפחה
ISRAEL CENTRAL COMMITTEE FOR TAHARAS HAMISHPACHA

JERUSALEM P.O.B. 5067 .ת.ד 285414 .טל, 28 ישא ברכה רח' ,ירושלים

This book is based on a manual for *Taharat HaMishpachah* teachers written in Hebrew by Mrs. Tehilla Abramov, which was published by our organization. We are proud and delighted to be part of this unique presentation to the English public, who will surely find much of interest in it.

The material printed was prepared in consultation with *gedolei hador*: our president HaGaon Rav Shlomo Zalman Auerbach *shlita*, and in certain matters, with HaGaon Rav Sholom Yosef Elyashiv *shlita*.

We have published many booklets on the subject of *Taharat HaMishpachah*, some of which have been printed in twelve languages and published in hundreds of thousands of copies.

Our monumental organization is the only one of its kind in Eretz Yisrael, and we specifically apply ourselves to the building and renovating of *mikvaot* in small settlements in cooperation and coordination with the government, for example the offices for Religious Affairs and Local Municipalities.

In addition, we have a special technical department (similar to a First Aid Department) for the daily repairing of *mikvaot*.

In addition to our written publications, we have a department for teaching and counselling which is staffed by hundreds of teachers and counsellors who make home visits, give classes and lectures, etc.

The existence of our organization is dependent solely on the generosity of fellow Jews throughout the world.

With multiple blessings from
the Holy City of Jerusalem

HaRav Yehoshua Levy
Director

In memory of my dear parents
לעילוי נשמות הורי היקרים

אבי מורי
ר' **ישראל אלכסנדר** ב"ר **חיים בן ציון
כץ** ז"ל
נלב"ע ט"ז אדר תשמ"ה
ת.נ.צ.ב.ה.

אמי מורתי
מרת רבקה ב"ר שלום כץ ע"ה
נלב"ע ז' מנחם אב תשי"ס
ת.נ.צ.ב.ה.

And in memory of my dear
parents in-law
לעילוי נשמות הורי בעלי היקרים

חמי מורי
ר' **אוריאל חיים** ב"ר **ישראל
אברמוב** ז"ל
נלב"ע ב' ניסן תשנ"ד
ת.נ.צ.ב.ה.

חמותי מורתי
מרת **חסיה** ב"ר **אברהם איסר
אברמוב** ע"ה
נלב"ע ב' תשרי תשנ"ב
ת.נ.צ.ב.ה.

Acknowledgments

My Thanks:

–to Mrs. Malka Touger, whose creative writing skills have enabled this book to emerge from my original Hebrew *Taharat HaMishpachah* teachers manual and lecture tapes into its present form.

–to all those whose encouragement was the force which made this book a reality.

With heartfelt gratitude to *Hashem Yisborach*,

Tehilla Abramov

Dedication

This book is dedicated

–to all the wonderful women in Eretz Yisrael and abroad whose authentic experiences appear in this book and which serve as an inspiration to us all. (For obvious reason, names and places, etc. have all been changed.)

–to all the *Taharat HaMishpachah* teachers and counsellors world-wide, whose sincere efforts have affected the lives of so many.

Tehilla Abramov
Nissan 5748

Although the Halachot in this book have been thoroughly checked by Rabbinical authorities, it is my fervent request that they be studied together with a Taharat HaMishpachah counsellor in order that all the details be fully understood.

With Thanks,

J. abramov

Tehilla Abramov

The
Secret of Jewish Femininity

Table of Contents

CHAPTER 1

The Secret of Jewish Femininity

SIMON'S GOOD FORTUNE had brought him through the
open door of one of the Warsaw Jewish community's
wealthiest, most generous households. Every evening, the
family and the many poor wayfarers invited as guests
would gather together for a sumptuous dinner.

Simon's mouth watered at the thought that he would
be able to partake of this feast. He had been away from
home for weeks, and many days had passed since he had
enjoyed a full meal. As he looked around the table, his
eyes widened at the exquisite furnishings and the
elegance.

Finally, it was time for the meal. The head of the
house rose from his place, removed a small crystal bell
from his pocket, and sounded it once. Servants quickly

appeared carrying trays laden with food. They graciously served all those assembled and returned to the kitchen.

When the first course was completed, the host again rang the bell. Servants reappeared, cleared off the tables, and returned shortly afterward with the second course. The same pattern was repeated each time. The host would ring the bell and, in response, servants would bring another course of delicacies.

Simon barely had time to savor the last bite of the delicious dessert when his host astounded all the guests by informing them that each one could take with him a gift. "You may choose anything you desire—one of the silver spoons, the crystal goblets, whatever you fancy," he announced.

Simon did not hesitate. One item alone had captured his attention. "If only I had a bell like that, I would never want for food," he thought. When Simon made his request, his host stared in disbelief. "Are you sure? There are much more valuable things in this house. Take a crystal goblet, a piece of silver. Why would you want the bell?" he asked.

But Simon couldn't be swayed. When he repeated his request, his host granted him his wish. Thanking him for his generosity, Simon placed the bell in his pocket and began his journey home. All along the way, he congratulated himself on his wise choice. "Never another worry about our next meal," he thought to himself.

Simon's wife had been anticipating his return. She had run out of supplies, and their creditors were hounding her to pay their long-overdue accounts. Simon, she hoped, would be returning with both money and supplies after having conducted business in the city.

When his wife sighted his approaching figure, she took heart at the obviously content look on her husband's face. "Simon, what have you brought home?" she asked impatiently after they had greeted each other.

"Don't worry, dear wife," he assured her. "This was a very successful trip. We'll never have to worry again. But I'll explain everything after dinner."

"What dinner!" his wife cried in dismay. "Whatever supplies you left ran out weeks ago. You didn't leave any money either. How am I supposed to make you dinner?"

He confidently beckoned his wife to join him at the table. With a serious and dignified look on his face, he rose, reached into his pocket, took out his crystal bell, and rang it gently.

His wife looked on in disbelief. Why would her husband ring the bell and then turn to the kitchen in anticipation? "What on earth is this all about?" she burst out in frustration.

Simon only shook his head in disappointment. "I don't understand," he mumbled to himself again and again. "It worked so well in the rich man's house..." (Dubno Maggid).

All of us occasionally make Simon's mistake of thinking we can have that which we desire without working for it. Recognizing this truth, that nothing worthwhile comes without effort, may make all the difference between a successful or failed marriage.

It is known that a woman's fundamental hope in life is that she will have a husband who loves her.

(The Steipler)

There isn't a girl who doesn't grow up with dreams of love and marriage. Every woman by nature looks forward to finding a man she can love and who will love her. She follows the prescribed path to marriage but often without too much thought about the deeper significance of what she is doing. Consequently, and sometimes only a few short months after the marriage ceremony, she wakes up and realizes that for a marriage to be meaningful and satisfying—for a marriage to work—"bell ringing" is not enough. Marriage is more than a ceremony. The glamor and glitter of the wedding soon become pictures in an album, and a woman confronts the need to relate beyond herself and give genuine love to a husband and a family. It is not long before the starry-eyed and blissful bride is jolted into the realization that for her marriage to grow into a success she must find a standard of values which will help her to understand what it means to be a woman, guide her in developing realistic expectations of married life, and make her aware of the depth of commitment she must make to marriage and family in order for them to work.

The story of the feminist movement in this generation is the story of women's struggle to orient themselves within a framework of such values. Women have made a courageous attempt to define their femininity and their identity within marriage and within society. They have experimented with many different approaches, some radically opposed to each other. But, today, most women still find themselves searching.

Feminism desires to reevaluate the way society under-stands femininity and womanhood. They declare, "We're dissatisfied with the role society has mapped out for us, and we want to arrive at a new definition." However, after more than twenty years of grappling with the issue, contemporary feminism has not offered a viable system of values. In fact, even as feminism has grown into a major force, morality has declined. The very institution of marriage is being questioned, the birth rate has plummeted, and women continue to feel that society is using and abusing them.

A pediatrician who accepted Torah practice after having been raised in a secular home disclosed to a friend, "I was religious for two years before I really believed in God."

Her listener was amazed: "How could you follow Torah laws if you didn't have that basic commitment?"

"I looked at families with Torah homes, and I saw their lifestyle. I was impressed with the women and felt they were more in touch with themselves than my contemporaries. Marriage wasn't a burden to them, but an expression of who they were. I became convinced that the excellent communication between husbands and wives and parents and children was a result of their Jewish practice. I wanted a home where these values could be realized. I wasn't going to allow my belief or lack of it to stand in the way."

The Torah system of values has produced families regarded as the epitome of stability and happiness for thousands of years. This has proven to be true whatever the society, whatever the culture Jews have found themselves a part of.

At no time has the contrast between the values Judaism stresses and those of the society around it been more pronounced than today. A look at the reasons for the sky-rocketing divorce rate tells part of the story.

Dr. Domeena Renshaw, head of the Sexual Dysfunction Clinic at Chicago's Loyola University, states that 80% of the divorces in Western society come about because of incompatibility within the couple's intimate lives. Furthermore, 50% of the couples who remain married have problems in this area.

Even without these statistics we can get an idea of the problem. The proliferation of clinics, specialists, manuals, and counselors, all offering the "secret" to problem-free intimate relations, attest to the difficulty modern society has in finding the proper balance within the realm of sexual relations.

This difficulty in building a balanced approach is an outgrowth of Western society's historical inability to come to terms with the issue of sexuality. Throughout history, we see two basic approaches:

–the worship of physical pleasure epitomized in the hedonism of Greek society. The pursuit of beauty and material enjoyment is looked on as an end in itself;

–the condemnation of sexuality epitomized in the asceticism of the early Christians. Sex is viewed as an expression of man's sinful nature.

It must be noted that both of these approaches view woman in a disparaging manner. For the Greeks, she was a sex object to be enjoyed and, then, discarded. For the Christians, woman is a temptress and source of desire. Marriage was accepted by the Christian world only as a way of controlling man's sinfulness. But the Christian ideal was and remains the celibate life.

Why hasn't Western man been able to rise above this unhealthy dichotomy? Because he operates from a materialistic perspective. This is the common point uniting the above approaches. Greek hedonism embraces materialism; Christian asceticism rejects it.

In contrast, Judaism operates from the view that the world is Godly, that God has vested it with an aspect of His creative potential. When we proclaim "Hear Israel, God is our Lord, God is One," we are not merely negating the existence of a second divinity; we are emphasizing how His transcendant Oneness pervades and permeates every aspect of the Creation. If this is true regarding the world at large, it must surely apply to the union between man and woman.

Know that the act of union is a holy and pure matter when carried out in the proper manner, at the proper time, and with the proper intentions. A person should not think there is anything degrading or unbecoming in the act of union, God forbid.

(Ramban, Iggeret HaKodesh)

Moreover, we see that the *Zohar* describes the union of a couple in marriage as the coming together of two half-souls. The physical union completes the expression of their total bond and, consequently, must be viewed as a Godly experience.

Such a perspective adds a new dimension to the woman's role. She is an equal partner in this holy activity. Her union with her husband is an opportunity for bringing another aspect of God's oneness into the world, the culmination of the love shared between them.

And he shall cling to his wife and they shall become one flesh.

(Bereshit 2:24)

The Hebrew word for love, *ahavah*, is numerically equivalent to *echad*, the Hebrew for one. Furthermore, when the two words' numerical values are added together, their sum is twenty-six. This is the numerical equivalent of God's name. Again, we see that, in Judaism, love is oneness, and when a couple join together in love, they reflect and reveal God's presence.

She should also join with him in holy and refined thoughts. Then, their minds will be fused as one...and they will both be united at this time, and God's Presence will rest between them.
(Ramban, Iggeret HaKodesh)

The idea that love is a holy affair is something intuitively understandable to a woman. In the morning, men recite the blessing *shelo asani ishah,* thanking God for "not making me a woman." However, women praise Him with the blessing *she'asani kirtzono,* for "making me according to His will." The commentaries explain that men recite this blessing in appreciation for the opportunity they have been given to fulfill more *mitzvot.* The Kabbalists add that the fact that women do not ask for the opportunity to perform more *mitzvot* is a reflection of their unique nature.

What is the intent of the *mitzvot?* to train our human natures to be attuned to God's will. Men are given more *mitzvot* because they require more training. Women by nature do not require as much "training," because they possess a natural, intuitive connection to God's will.

Surely, woman's clearer understanding of God's will is reflected in her approach to sexuality. She has been granted a natural ability to appreciate marital intimacy as holy and divine. Therefore, the merely physical is often not sufficient for her. In order to function as a total woman, she must feel that intimacy is more than a physical act. It must involve her soul and provide her with deep emotional fulfillment.

Rashi explains that women have a greater potential for sexual desire than men (*Bereshit* 3:16). This desire is not simply for the physical activity, but for the act of holiness and love described above.

This recognition of a woman's sexuality is the cornerstone of the system of values and laws referred to as *Taharat HaMishpachah,* the Godly system governing marital relations. The Torah describes the mitzvah of marital intimacy as *onah,* "a response to her," implying that a man must attune himself to his wife and her desire for holiness in the marriage.

The conception of sexuality as a holy function requires that it be carried out within the context of guidelines es-tablished by God. As will be explained, these guidelines, the "whens" and "when nots" of *Taharat HaMishpachah,* follow a woman's own natural rhythms and inclinations and reflect her desire for both privacy and individuality, closeness and love.

Taharat HaMishpachah is the secret of Jewish femininity. It provides a couple with a divinely ordained framework showing them how to relate to each other and express and build their love and devotion. On this sturdy foundation, they can construct a superstructure of family and home. The study of these ideas and their application within the context of our lives will help each of us discover insights which are old, for they were given by God on Mount Sinai, but new, for they are continually relevant to our lives as women and as Jews.

CHAPTER 2

The Changing Status

SANDRA, 21, AND BRIAN, 24, had been dating for a number of years while attending college in Southern California. The summer after graduation, they decided to get married. The couple set a date for their wedding for eight weeks later. As their families wanted a traditional ceremony, Brian and Sandra chose an orthodox rabbi to officiate. But, as the two now freely admit, the choice of rabbi really made no difference to them. With casual indifference, Brian and Sandra arrived at the Rabbi's house for an appointment. The Rabbi greeted them warmly and invited them into his study.

"Congratulations on your engagement," he smiled at the couple. "I'd be pleased to officiate at your wedding. But, I want you to understand that a Jewish marriage is not a casual matter. There's a lot involved...."

"He's trying to explain why he is going to ask for a high fee," Brian mused to himself. "It's okay, Rabbi," he cut him off. "You don't have to worry about the fee."

"No, I'm not talking about my fee or even the ceremony itself. In Judaism, a marriage is more than standing together at the altar. I invited you over to share some thoughts and insights on the way Judaism looks at marriage."

"Oh, no!" groaned Brian to himself, as the Rabbi paused for a moment. "I bet we're in for a sermon...."

"I thought we were just going to finalize details," thought Sandra. "Now, we have to sit through a lecture...."

They gave each other a glance of mutual resolve: They would endure this ordeal with respect and understanding. This would be their first and last visit to the Rabbi.

"You must both be very preoccupied with wedding preparations," the Rabbi said. "I appreciate your coming despite your busy schedules. You see, we too often concern ourselves solely with wedding preparations while overlooking the need to prepare for the marriage itself.

"The books on those shelves," the Rabbi continued, pointing to several large volumes, "talk about marriage. Not the ceremony, but what comes afterwards—in particular, the subjects of intimate relations and husband and wife interaction."

Brian's ears perked up. His mind had been wandering. What was this Rabbi saying? A Rabbi talking about sex?

"When a couple is united in marriage, they join in a bond of holiness," the Rabbi was saying. "Judaism does not view intimacy as removed from holiness. On the contrary, it is a vital area of life where God becomes part of our existence in a very real way. The greatest Sages of the Talmud would teach their daughters how to attract their husbands...."

Sandra shifted uneasily in her chair. She felt her face redden. "I can't believe it," she thought to herself. "On the campus, we discuss sex freely, but I never imagined a Rabbi would confront the subject with such a matter-of-fact approach!" She decided to pay closer attention.

Noticing her interest, the Rabbi continued: "There is much this lifestyle has to offer to both partners, but I believe my wife would be better able to explain the details to you, Sandra, than I would." He gestured toward an attractively dressed woman who had been busy in the adjoining room.

Sandra sighed, "I hope I'm not going to get a quick course on preparing gefilte fish and matza balls! Just when things are getting interesting, I'm being sent off to the 'Rebbetzin.'" Reluctantly, she joined the Rabbi's wife in the living room.

In fact, their conversation involved far more than simply a cooking lesson. For the first time in her life, Sandra heard an orthodox Jewish woman talk openly about physical relations. Sandra was amazed at the familiarity and ease with which the Rebbetzin discussed matters which she thought were taboo and improper for observant people.

"You mean this is actually mentioned in the Bible?" she asked in surprise.

"Of course!" came the reply. "God created our bodies. He put the capacity to love in our hearts. Isn't it logical to assume that He also wanted to teach man (and woman!) how and whom to love?"

That first chat turned out to be just the beginning. What was meant to be a one-time encounter turned into a series of sessions spent with the Rabbi and his wife learning the system of *Taharat HaMishpachah*. Abstention from physical contact between husband and wife during menstruation and for the seven days following, and immersion in the *mikvah*, were presented not only as a Godly command, but also as a practice leading to personal growth and marital happiness.

Brian's parents were divorced. He deeply wanted his marriage to succeed and soon realized that the ideas being presented to him anticipated and answered his concerns. The Torah's approach to marriage convinced him of the need to study and discover more of what Judaism had to offer.

Sandra sensed a new dimension in her anticipation of their upcoming wedding. She began to feel that a Torah lifestyle would enhance her ability to express her femininity, whereas the values modern society held out as the ideal for women ignored this aspect of her personality.

Looking back, Sandra remembers that hard beginning with a chuckle. "After a couple of weeks, we agreed to bear with separation till the wedding. Brian had to drive me to my parents' home every night." He would plead to hold Sandra's hand for just a little while, but Sandra wouldn't budge. "I can't touch you, and I won't until the wedding!"

The highlight of this new experience was her immersion in the *mikvah*. "I can't describe the feeling. All I can say is that it made it all very, very special." Sandra's going to the *mikvah* was not a one-time affair. She is delighted to be able to recapture the feeling periodically, for both she and Brian have committed themselves to keeping a Jewish home.

"At first, Brian was hesitant. He didn't really believe we could do it. But now, well, it's grown on us, and we've grown through it. I look at some of my college friends, who are still searching for a deeper sense of meaning in their relationships, and say to myself, 'There, but for the grace of God (and the Rabbi's wife!) go I.'"

Sandra and Brian were fortunate. They recognized that the marriage bonds between a man and his wife present an opportunity to introduce an added measure of holiness into one's life, even into that area which is most intimate. By allowing this holiness into their marriage, a man and wife will immeasurably strengthen their relationship.

A line connecting two points is easily broken, whereas a triangle is the sturdiest geometric form. Similarly, a marriage must be more than a bond between man and woman. We need a third partner—God. The Master of the universe, the Creator of all beings, designed a unique plan for achieving the maximum joy and fulfillment that marriage can offer. The laws of *Taharat HaMishpachah* provide the framework for this plan.

The laws of *Taharat HaMishpachah* revolve around the intimate relationship between man and wife. A man and woman make a mutual commitment to fulfill these commandments—to express their love and affection for one another within the rhythms of the woman's physical cycle. During the days of the month when a woman has her menstrual period, she is considered a *niddah*. The root of this Hebrew word is *nadad*—to separate. While a *niddah*, a woman separates from her husband. As her physical state changes, she prepares herself emotionally and spiritually for the time when she and her husband will be together again. After immersion in a *mikvah*, the couple are reunited in a spirit of holiness and love.

The observance of the laws of *Taharat HaMishpachah* strengthens every Jewish marriage. Moreover, the care with which they have been followed has been one of the major factors ensuring the survival of our people. The faithful practice of these laws throughout the generations has added link after link in Judaism's golden chain.

We inherited the commitment to keep these laws, even under the most trying circumstances, from our ancestors in ancient Egypt. Enslaved and compelled to perform hard labor, the men's spirits soon faltered. They no longer desired marital relations. They could not bear to see the children they conceived flung into the roaring waters of the Nile river. In desperation, they avoided their wives, unwilling to bring further sorrow upon their families.

It was the women who were filled with hope and belief. Their inner strength inspired them to seek out their husbands and encourage them to father a next generation regardless of their present hardships. These women observed the laws of Family Purity in the depths of slavery, determined that the Jewish nation would carry on.

When the women prepared to be with their husbands, they took great pains to beautify themselves and appear attractive. Lacking even the most basic cosmetic tools, they used copper plaques for mirrors. With prayers in their hearts, they scrubbed the copper till it shone in order that they could see their reflections.

Our Sages declared that the Jewish people were redeemed from Egypt in the merit of those righteous women. It was because the women recognized the holiness inherent in marital relations and family life in general that they were able to persevere and raise a new generation that would emerge a new nation: the Jewish people.

Their commitment was not forgotten. At the giving of the Torah on Mount Sinai, God commanded the Jewish people to build a Sanctuary. Every individual was anxious to contribute to the fashioning of this holy structure. In addition to gifts of gold and silver, the women donated their prized personal possessions: those handmade copper mirrors.

Moshe Rabbenu was reluctant to accept such a contribution. He questioned the mirrors' apparent lack of holiness and refinement. Their purpose was so clearly physically oriented. Noticing his indecision, God revealed Himself to Moshe: "Take them. They're dearer to Me than anything else." God instructed Moshe to melt the copper plaques and construct the basin used in the Sanctuary from that very metal. Before the priests began their service in the Sanctuary, they would wash from this basin, reminding themselves of the unique dedication of the Jewish women, for it was they who understood that holiness in religious life cannot be separated from holiness in family life (*Rashi, Shemot* 38:8).

Every practice for which Israel has sacrificed itself has been maintained.

(Mechilta, Ki Tissah)

There are no other *mitzvot* that have proven such a challenge to women as those surrounding the observance of

Taharat HaMishpachah. The determination of our fore-mothers in Egypt is but one example. Throughout the generations, Jewish women have provided us with a legacy of strength and courage in their observance of the laws of *Taharat HaMishpachah.* Recent archaeological discoveries at Masada, for instance, indicate that the Jewish defenders of that clifftop site maintained an extensive system of *mikvaot.* Even in the midst of a life-and-death struggle, they never lost sight of exactly what they were fighting for.

But we needn't even go back that far to find examples of brave determination to follow God's will....

"You ask why I am crying?" exclaims a newly arrived immigrant from behind the iron curtain. Seated in the comfortable waiting room of an attractive *mikvah* building in Eretz Yisrael, Mrs. Krovsky wipes a tear from her eye as she relates her experiences to the *mikvah* attendant.

"It's less than a month since we left Russia. This is the first time I'm going to the *mikvah* without worrying who is looking over my shoulder.

"There are hundreds of women in Russia who keep *Taharat HaMishpachah.* It is extremely difficult, especially if you have young children and you work outside your home. My sixteen years of married life were a story of hiding, secrecy, and fear. Going to a *mikvah* was always a logistical nightmare. Where to go? How to get there? How to avoid suspicion? How to meet the travel expenses?

"You can't imagine the commitment marriage demands from an observant Jew in Russia. While most brides were concerned with wedding preparations, I was preoccupied with constructing a plan of action to make observing *Taharat HaMishpachah* feasible. My hometown did not have a *mikvah*; the nearest one was in Chernowitz, eighty kilometers away."

Shortly after the birth of Mrs. Krovsky's first daughter, the *mikvah* and the adjoining shul in Chernowitz were closed down. Desperate inquiries led to the discovery of an "officially permitted" *mikvah* in Lemberg, 115 kilometers away. Mrs. Krovsky would go to work in the morning as usual, then travel to Lemberg by bus or train in the afternoon. "I had to make the return trip late the same night in order to report to work the next morning on time. Otherwise, people would begin asking questions.

"These were considered 'ideal conditions.' The real difficulties started when the Lemberg *mikvah* was also shut down. We turned back to Chernowitz where a group of dedicated Jews tried to re-open an old *mikvah* dating back to pre-war times. This *mikvah* was located in the basement of a private home. Its owner, a Jewish woman, was reluctant to endanger herself and others by allowing access to the much sought-after pool in her basement. Many hours of imploring and pleading and, of course, the promise of a handsome fee finally persuaded her to agree.

"The next step was to repair the old *mikvah* and prepare it for use. All the construction had to be carried out in maximum secrecy and silence. We could not risk talkative neighbors. The woman would not allow us to build an entrance from her home. The only way to get in was by crawling through a hole in the basement wall.

"Despite the generous sum of money the house owner received, she would not allow the use of the *mikvah* on Sundays and public holidays. On these days, she ran an active 'black market' in her home, and she didn't want visitors to inquire about the strange figures emerging from the cellar.

"Still, we insisted on using the *mikvah* on those days, promising to stay out of sight of her customers. I remember many an anxious hour, waiting patiently by the exit, praying that the last buyer would leave in time for me to make the last train home."

Years passed, and another old basement *mikvah* became available in the center of town. At first, the water was heated by a boiler, but tenants complained about the unexplainable rise in the electric bill. For fear of discovery, the electric wiring to the *mikvah* was disconnected. "I don't have to tell you how cold water can get in the freezing Russian winter. We were forced to heat up water on gas stoves upstairs and carry it down to the basement, tens of buckets each time."

When this was no longer feasible, Mrs. Krovsky tried a different alternative, a 450-kilometer trip across the Carpathian mountains to the city of Ungrod. Sometimes she was lucky enough to make the trip by plane. Usually, she would fly one way and take a bus home. "I still shudder at the thought of those terrifying late-night bus rides among the primitive Russian peasants.

"When we could afford a vacation to the big cities— Moscow, Leningrad, or Kiev—I had the opportunity to use the local *mikvah*. It was sad to behold the small number of women who took advantage of the *mikvah*.

Many were afraid to come lest they be questioned—even the attendants could have been informers.

"Thank God, that's all past history. Here in Eretz Yisrael, I can fulfill the vital mitzvah of *Taharat Ha-Mishpachah* in comfort and ease. Do you still wonder why I am tearful?"

The Russian woman's story can be retold with different names and in different places—wherever there is a Jewish woman determined to maintain the practice of *Taharat Ha-Mishpachah.*

In southern Spain, a small port city located between mountain and sea lies basking in the Mediterranean sun. The peaceful vacation atmosphere of this resort town belies the constant struggle of one observant Jewish family to keep Torah and *mitzvot,* and to share our singular heritage with other Jews. Their house is always full of guests, and many travelers to Spain have returned home inspired to seek out their Jewish heritage because of the experience they shared with the Gold family.

In addition to the lack of suitable schools, kosher food, and active synagogue, there is no *mikvah.* Regular flights to France with a nursing infant are not feasible. Besides, what would Mrs. Gold's husband do with their five other young children at home? The only alternative is the sea. Spain's beaches are extremely inviting on hot, sunny summer days, but nighttime dipping (especially in the winter) is not everyone's delight. Nevertheless, once a month Mrs. Gold makes her way across the sandy beach, prepared to endure the chilly waters and all the while careful to abide by the specific laws of using the sea for immersion.

Even under conditions of freedom, acceptance, and affluence, adhering to the dictates of *Taharat HaMishpachah* can prove to be a challenge—a point Mrs. Gold could freely attest to. The stories of women who have persevered in the face of great hardship may appear to dwarf our own difficulties, but each woman can relate her own stories of heroic determination and unswerving commitment to fulfill God's will.

The Jewish woman has been charged with the responsibility for the maintenance of this fundamental mitzvah. While there are laws and prohibitions, such as observing the *harchakot*, the laws of separation, for which the husband, too, is responsible, the practical observance of this mitzvah—checking her body, immersing in the *mikvah*, and keeping a calendar—is entrusted solely to the Jewish woman. No one is instructed to verify or check her actions. Her word is relied upon absolutely, and halachic decisions are based on information which she provides.

The Jewish woman deserves this trust. Not only because it's her body which is involved, but also because God esteems women's ability to keep the Torah. "Thus shall you say to the house of Yaacov and tell to the children of Israel" (*Shemot* 19:3). "The house of Yaacov" refers to the Jewish women, and, yet, we see that Moshe Rabbenu was instructed to teach the Torah to them before the men. Clearly, when it comes to keeping the Torah, women's integrity is not in doubt.

Rabbi Levi Yitzchak of Berditchev was famous for his constant efforts to find merit in and glorify his Jewish brethren. Once, on the day before Passover, he sent his attendant in search of a pint of beer. The attendant knocked on the doors of the freshly cleaned Jewish homes and stated his request.

"What?" came the replies. "Beer! Beer is *chametz*! Tonight is Passover, and I have already cleaned my home. God forbid we should possess a drop of *chametz* at this hour!" The attendant returned empty-handed to Rabbi Levi Yitzchak, regretful that he could not fulfill his Rebbe's wishes.

Rabbi Levi Yitzchak seemed rather pleased. He sent the attendant out once again, this time to fetch a bit of tobacco from any one of the Jews in the village. Government officials had recently forbidden possession of tobacco and threatened to imprison anyone found with it. To enforce their edict, they would make surprise searches among the villagers.

Nevertheless, the attendant had little difficulty obtaining this forbidden item. He handed Rabbi Levi Yitzchak the package, but instead of smoking the tobacco, Rabbi Levi Yitzchak waved it towards the heavens. Lifting his eyes and with a beaming look of pride on his face, he exclaimed, "God, see how precious Your commandments are to Your children! The government posts soldiers to enforce its rules and regulations, yet see how easily I was able to procure this tobacco. Almost four thousand years ago, You commanded the Jewish people to rid their homes of *chametz*. Today, not a drop could be found! Your people keep Your commandments sincerely without any pressure or force."

It is part of the pride of our heritage that no matter how complex or difficult the keeping of a mitzvah may be, the Jewish people have demonstrated incredible integrity in their standards of observance. Therefore, the trust the Torah places with women in the matter of *Taharat HaMishpachah* is nothing out of the ordinary. In fact, it is just another indication of how highly the Torah regards them.

The Torah has placed a great responsibility in the hands of women. However, this responsibility should not create undue anxiety or tension. A joyful approach to observing the rules of *Taharat HaMishpachah* invites the *Shechinah*, God's Presence, to descend upon the couple.

"When a man and woman merit it, the *Shechinah* rests between them" (*Sotah* 17a). The letters of the Hebrew word for woman, *ishah,* contain the word *eish,* meaning fire. The letters of the word *ish,* the Hebrew for man, also contain *eish* —fire. The two remaining letters contained in each of their names, *yud* and *heh,* combine to form God's name, *Yud-Heh*. Thus, when a man and a woman approach marriage in the proper way, God's Presence rests between them, but if they remove Godliness (God's name) from their marriage, they are left with fire—*eish*. Their marriage will be as vulnerable as dry straw before a flame. The "proper way" calls for a correct attitude. Our Sages declared, "The *Shechinah* rests only in an atmosphere of joy" (*Shabbat* 30b). The Talmud encourages a couple to fulfill the *mitzvot* associated with *Taharat HaMishpachah* with happiness and joy. In this manner, Godliness becomes a very real force in our lives, not only in the synagogue, or in those areas of life which we consider holy, but in every aspect of our life experience.

Mrs. Bernstein is an observant woman. In addition to managing her home and caring for her children, she has established a growing business as an interior decorating consultant. Stressing sensitivity and the personal touch, she involves herself in her clients' needs and requirements by sharing her insights on the best ways to set up a Jewish home.

She recalls one particularly inquisitive woman who was impressed with this professional, yet personal approach. As the two women chatted over tea, Mrs. Bernstein suggested a variety of attractive decorating plans.

Their conversation continued, as Mrs. Bernstein described to her client the transformation of a house into a home. She stressed the importance and impact that proper decor can have on creating a Jewish atmosphere within the walls of the home.

"And in the bedroom..." she continued.

"In the bedroom!" exclaimed her client. "I can understand your concern with religion in the kitchen, dining room, and children's room. I agree to make room for God in my home. He's welcome on the doorposts and in the living room. But is He really interested in our private bedroom?"

"Surely," smiled Mrs. Bernstein, "every aspect of our lives should be permeated with our Jewishness. Tell me, would you like to leave God out of the bedroom? It is precisely this area that becomes the center of so much marital friction. Here, God's directives and the holiness and sanctity they produce are most necessary."

Mrs. Bernstein concluded with a twinkle in her eye: "I've drawn up a plan for your bedroom with two separate beds. Our Sages stated, 'When man and woman merit, the Divine Presence rests between them.' If a couple want God's Presence in their house, they must also make room for it in the bedroom."

The rules of *Taharat HaMishpachah* are designed to sustain and preserve the original bond that began under the marriage canopy. While a woman is a *niddah*, she does not have any physical contact with her husband. This period of physical separation is accompanied by psychological and spiritual preparation and, finally, sanctification, as she immerses in the *mikvah*. Only then may marital relations be resumed. One of the greatest dangers to a satisfying and fulfilling marriage is sexual boredom. The initial excitement of romance and discovery ebbs with time. When a couple keep the laws of *Taharat HaMishpachah*, the original love and excitement they shared is renewed each month.

Even from a purely medical perspective, observing *Taharat HaMishpachah* can be beneficial. Research shows that, generally, a woman's vaginal discharge is mildly acidic and, therefore, antiseptic. In contrast, at the time of her period, this discharge is alkaline and it takes approximately seven days to regain its normal pH. Thus, during this time, the vagina lacks its natural protection and the possibility of infection rises.

Furthermore, at the time of menstruation, the uterine lining has been shed and the entire uterine channel resembles an open wound. This leaves it susceptible to the entrance of germs. It takes seven days after the end of the period for the lining to become firm and strong again. Intimate relations during the time the Torah defines as *niddah* may then prove harmful.

Finally, a number of medical studies of the incidence of cervical cancer show that it can occur as much as twenty times more frequently among women who don't practice *Taharat HaMishpachah* than among those who do.

"I am God who heals you" (*Shemot* 15:26). God has given us the Torah's guidelines as a way of life and has promised that fulfilling its commandments will lead to a lifetime of health and prosperity. Nevertheless, we must remember that the reason for observing the *mitzvot* is not the benefits we will reap from them, but that they are God's will.

While the observance of *Taharat HaMishpachah* makes sense medically as well as sexually, the very name *Taharat HaMishpachah—Family* Purity—would imply that its merit extends far beyond these two areas. It is not called *Taharat HaIshah*, 'woman's' purity, despite its obvious connection with a woman's cycle; not just the woman herself, but her immediate and extended family, the entire Jewish nation and its future generations, are directly influenced by the purity and wholesomeness which the Divine plan inspires.

Rav Chalaftah declared: "How fortunate is the woman! How fortunate is the mother! How fortunate is the family of any woman who keeps the laws properly."

(Niddah 4:1)

Taharat HaMishpachah is influential in molding the spiritual nature and well-being of our children. We all want the best for our offspring. Keeping *Taharat HaMishpachah* is something we can do for them even before conception.

Room 312 on the third floor of Rambam Hospital in Haifa was occupied by two middle-aged Israeli men, Mr. Ben-Shalom, the secretary of one of Israel's more successful kibbutzim, and Mr. Ganon, the owner of a large import-export concern. The two had much in common. They had both lived in Israel since before 1948 and witnessed the country's birth and phenomenal development.

They spent many hours in conversation. Mr. Ganon was impressed with his roommate's popularity. It seemed that everyone on the kibbutz came to visit him. Two young men, in particular, attracted Mr. Ganon's attention. They visited frequently, and Mr. Ben-Shalom seemed very pleased to see them.

They appeared so different from the others. Mr Ben-Shalom's kibbutz belonged to Kibbutz HaArtzi, the secular-left kibbutz movement. These youths wore *kippot* on their heads and sported unshaven sideburns and *tzitzit*. Where did they meet Mr. Ben-Shalom? How did the apparent closeness between them develop?

One day, Mr. Ganon could not contain his curiosity any longer. "Excuse me for being so nosy," he remarked to Mr. Ben-Shalom, "but who are those two young orthodox fellows who visit you so often?"

Mr. Ben-Shalom smiled and propped his cushions up behind him. "They're two of the kibbutz's prize products, but to understand how this came to be is a long story."

Mr. Ganon turned to his friend attentively, and Mr. Ben-Shalom continued:

"During the Holocaust," he began, "a mother and daughter, the sole survivors of an entire family, were deported to a Nazi death camp. They clung together as their train was unloaded. Some passengers were sent to the gas chambers immediately, others to the barracks.

"As the mother was torn away from her daughter, she implored her: 'Promise me that if you survive and live to marry and build a home, you will keep *Taharat Ha-Mishpachah.*'

"With tears in her eyes, the girl vowed to fulfill her mother's last wish. She had no idea of their meaning, but she repeated the words *Taharat HaMishpachah* over and over again, engraving them in her mind, lest she forget. She sensed their message as her only connection to a world that no longer existed....

"What she endured, how she endured, is too long a story, but she made it. When the war was over, she was sent to Israel by the Jewish Agency Committee for Refugees. Here, she was placed in our kibbutz and soon acclimated herself to her new life.

"Years passed. When she graduated from university, her boyfriend from the kibbutz proposed marriage. It was then that she remembered her mother's last wish. The words *Taharat HaMishpachah* echoed in her ears, and she was determined to keep the promise she had made.

" 'I hope you will agree to my condition,' she said to him, relating her vow. 'I don't even know what *Taharat HaMishpachah* is, but I have decided to keep it!'

"Impressed with her sincerity, he agreed, and the girl set about seeking an explanation on the subject. She received individual instruction and learned the detailed laws. The more she learned, the happier she felt with her decision. Sensing a new connection with her long-gone

family, her past, and her people's history, she approach-
ed marriage with confidence and joy.

"The couple continued to live on the kibbutz. Nothing
differentiated them from the other *chaverim* except for a
deep and lasting commitment to the observance of
Taharat HaMishpachah."

Mr. Ben-Shalom paused. His roommate eyed him
curiously, sensing there was more to come.

"You see, my friend," he continued, "that Holocaust
survivor is my wife, and those two boys are our sons.
They are the envy of all my friends. Everyone is impressed by their refinement, character, and their desire
for meaning and direction in life. All the *kibbutznikkim*
respect them for their observant lifestyle. I believe it has
something to do with the commitment my wife and I
made."

CHAPTER 3

Getting to Know Yourself

"HIS HEAD IS as the most fine gold, his locks are wavy, black as a raven's" (*Shir HaShirim* 5:11). Our Sages noted that the Hebrew word for raven, *orev*, resembles the Hebrew for sweet, *arev*. They commented: There are certain passages of the Torah, for example, the laws of *niddah*, which may appear too ugly and black to teach publicly. Nevertheless, God declares, "To Me, they are as sweet as fine gold."

The laws of *niddah* require a familiarity with the intimate details of our bodies. That these details should be discussed, and in the open at that, can be an uncomfortable thought. Nevertheless, God treasures the study and examination of them, because only through such study is it possible to fulfill the laws properly

What Is the Law of a *Niddah?*

The Torah states that a woman becomes *teme'ah*, ritually impure, when she experiences her menstrual period, and prohibits intimacy with a woman while she is in this state (*VaYikra* 18:19-24). The Torah prescribes the punishment of *karet* for violation of this prohibition, the same punishment that is prescribed for a person who is not circumcised or who eats on Yom Kippur.

Tumah, ritual impurity, and *taharah*, ritual purity, are spiritual concepts. To quote the Rambam: "It is clear that the laws of ritual purity and impurity are decrees of the Torah that cannot be comprehended by human wisdom" (*Hilchot Mikvaot* 11:12). In no manner or form can they be identified with physical cleanliness and its opposite. Before immersing herself in the *mikvah*, a woman cleanses herself thoroughly. Nevertheless, to become ritually pure, she must immerse in the *mikvah's* waters. Similarly, the High Priest would immerse himself in the *mikvah* five times on Yom Kippur. Surely these immersions were not required because he was dirty!

The laws of *Taharat HaMishpachah* are designed to be in harmony with a woman's physical, emotional, spiritual, and psychological makeup. They allow and require her to be "in touch" with herself in a very real and conscious manner.

When Does a Woman Enter the State of *Niddah*?

Any woman—even if she be pregnant, nursing, or past menopause—who discovers a discharge of blood which originated from her uterus enters the state of *niddah*. This applies whether the discharge occurs at a time when she would normally expect her period or not. Uterine bleeding resulting from birth or a gynecologist's examination also renders a woman a *niddah*. So does hymenal bleeding.

A woman must be aware of the laws governing this subject so that she will be knowledgeable enough to detect the possibility of her being a *niddah*. God placed the responsibility of observing the laws of *Taharat HaMishpachah* in the woman's hands. She must know when she becomes a *niddah* and when she is *tehorah*, i.e., not a *niddah*.

Nevertheless, meeting this responsibility requires the assistance and guidance of a Rav. In addition to his halachic knowledge, a Rav will have developed the sensitivity required for dealing with these delicate and personal issues. A woman must have a Rav with whom she feels comfortable to consult when questions arise.

How Does One Determine the State of *Niddah*?

Torah law distinguishes between two types of discharges:

1. a *mareh*, in which the discharge is accompanied by a specific physical sensation;
2. a *ketem*, in which a stain is discovered without any prior sensation.

A *mareh* always renders a woman a *niddah*. Even the tiniest drop of blood coming from the uterus places a woman in that state. In contrast, there are certain leniencies in regard to *ketamim*. The stains must be brought to a Rav who will decide the matter according to criteria discussed later. Blood which is discovered in the process of a *bedikah*, an internal examination, is considered equivalent to a *mareh*.

Our Sages determined two criteria for defining the term "physical sensation":

1. a sensation of the opening of the uterus (it is very rare for a woman to be able to distinguish this feeling nowadays);
2. the feeling of liquid passing from the vagina.

A woman who experiences either of these sensations is required to check herself shortly afterwards by means of a *bedikah* cloth in order to verify whether the feeling was connected with uterine bleeding or not. (How the *bedikah* is performed is explained in chap. 5.)

If she discovers blood, she becomes a *niddah*. If she discovers a secretion whose color clearly indicates that it is not blood (see below), she is *tehorah*. If she does not discover any secretion at all, she should consult a Rav. This *bedikah* does not have to be made by women who are more than three months pregnant, women who have not menstruated while nursing, or women who are past menopause.

Similarly, a woman who frequently experiences vaginal discharges other than blood may avoid the need for constant internal examinations by carrying out the following procedure:

On three successive occasions, shortly after the sensation of vaginal flow, the woman should make a *bedikah*. If she discovers secretions other than blood, she may rest assured that, in her case, this sensation is not necessarily related to the onset of menstruation.

With this procedure, a woman establishes that her vaginal discharges are normally not blood. Hence, she is never required to check for uterine bleeding after experiencing such a sensation again unless it occurs on the days on which she might expect her menstrual period.

Determining the Nature of a Vaginal Discharge

A discharge of a color other than white, blue, or green may render a woman a *niddah*. In the event of the discovery of discharges of questionable colors, she should consult a Rav to determine her status. It is not sufficient to consult one's husband or a friend, even if they are somewhat knowledgeable concerning these matters.

Staining

A woman may discover a *ketem*, stain, of a questionable color resembling blood without experiencing any sensation associated with vaginal discharge. This might render her a *niddah*, and she must consult a Rav to determine her status. It is preferable to consult the Rav as soon as possible.

Among the factors which are important in facilitating the Rav's decision are

1.   where the stain was found: on the woman's body (where on the body?), on her clothes (where on the clothes? were they white or colored? outer clothes or underclothes?), or on her sheets (were they white or colored?);

2.   the color of the stain;

3.   the cleanliness of the place where the stain was found;

4. the possibility of attributing the stain to external factors (e.g., a mother treating a child's nosebleed, a mosquito bite, preparation of red colored foods);

5. the size of the stain.

A *ketem* can only render a woman a *niddah* if it is a *gris* in size. The latter measurement is the size of a circle approximately nineteen millimeters in diameter (similar to the size of an Israeli telephone token or an American dime). However, it is rare to find stains so conveniently circular. The particular rules of measuring the size of a different shaped stain, what to do when two or smaller stains are discovered next to each other, and other particular questions make the guidance of a Rav a necessity.

It must be emphasized that the above applies to stains discovered on the body or on clothes without experiencing any sensations associated with vaginal discharge. When a stain is discovered on a *bedikah* cloth (see chap. 5), more stringent rules apply, and even the tiniest drop of blood can render a woman a *niddah*.

General Rules Regarding Stains

1. Do not make internal inspections after discovering a stain unless instructed to do so by a Rav.

2. It is a good idea to wear colored underwear when *tehorah*. This minimizes the possibility that any given stain will render a woman a *niddah*.

3. Do not inspect toilet paper after use.

4. Stains are not regarded as contributing factors in calculating *onot* (see chap. 10).

Gynecological Examinations

Uterine bleeding resulting from a gynecologist's internal examination renders a woman a *niddah*. Furthermore, in certain instances, this examination may render a woman a *niddah* even if no bleeding is apparent. This matter can only be decided by a Rav. However, awareness of the nature of the examination can greatly assist a woman and her Rav in determining her status. It is suggested that these guidelines be followed:

1. A gynecologist's examinations should ideally be scheduled for the period when a woman is a *niddah* and before she makes a *hefsek taharah*, confirmation of the end of menstrual flow (see chap. 5).

2. Inquire about the nature and necessity of the examination beforehand.

3. After the examination, request complete details about the procedure. In particular, if a wound is discovered, find out its exact location.

4. A manual examination which does not penetrate the uterus itself does not make a woman a *niddah*. Examinations using certain instruments may cause the opening up of the uterus and, thus, render a woman a *niddah*. To give a judgement on this matter, a Rav must be informed about which instruments were used.

5. Needless to say, a gynecologist's opinion without the confirmation of a rabbinic authority may not be relied upon in determining a woman's *niddah* status.

Situations that require consultation with both medical and halachic authorities include

a)   blood found in urine;
b)   a sore in the vaginal area;
c)   cervical erosion or other internal bleeding;
d)   midcycle bleeding and staining.

The Role of the Rav

A Rav was seated in the study of a shul in a small shtetel in Eastern Europe surrounded by students eager to hear his explanation of the Talmud. His lecture was suddenly interrupted when a woman knocked on the door and asked the Rav whether she could ask his opinion on a pressing *she'elah* (halachic question).

The Rav nodded in acquiescence, and the woman began to relate her story. The students all listened carefully, wondering what the problem would be and how their teacher would respond.

"Oh, revered Rabbi," she began, "after I kashered my chicken for Shabbat and cooked it, I set it on the window sill to cool. I was about to start baking my kugel when I noticed that one of the chicken's bones was broken in a place which might render it *trefe* [unfit to eat]. I was about to bring it to the Rav to check when..."

The woman paused for a moment to catch her breath, looking around at her attentive audience. "Then, before I could stop him," she said, wringing her hands in despair, "my pet cat spotted the chicken and devoured it. I didn't have a chance to snatch it away."

The Rav listened patiently, wondering what the question was, but the woman was too distraught to continue. "What is your question, my good woman?" he asked gently.

"Oh, respected Rabbi," she blurted out, "I had just fed my cat a bowl of milk! Now, he consumed a chicken. What must I do? May I still keep him as a mice chaser in my kosher household?"

The students struggled to contain their laughter. But they were amazed at the Rav's reaction. His face took on a serious look as he delved into his books pretending to research the question. He turned the pages back and forth as if in the midst of an issue of the greatest importance. Knitting his brow, he suddenly rose from his seat, climbed onto a stool, and reached for a book from a high shelf. He leafed through it hurriedly, making believe he was looking for a specific chapter.

After a few minutes of "research," he seem satisfied and turned to the woman. "My good woman," he said in an authoritative voice, "your cat must be considered *trefe*. Nevertheless, you may keep him as a mice chaser. May I suggest that in the future you cool your cooked chickens out of his reach so as not to suffer a loss."

Much relieved, the woman thanked the Rav for his advice and left the study. The students began to giggle, but contained themselves because of the serious, but satisfied, look on their teacher's face. One of them respectfully asked the Rav why he troubled himself so much with the foolish question. "Had I rebuked that woman or caused her any uneasiness," the Rav replied, "it is very probable that she would hesitate to approach me in the future with an issue that is halachically important. I wanted to show her that her problem was worthy of attention. She left feeling satisfied and will return if she has any further 'questions' in the future."

That shtetel Rav serves as a fine example of the sensitivity and concern for the individual that a Rav must possess in addition to his halachic knowledge. This is particularly important in regard to *Taharat HaMishpachah*. The Rav is accustomed to dealing with the issue in a sensitive fashion, conscious of the delicacy of the issues involved and concerned for the woman's need for privacy.

Some of the questions he asks may cause some embarrassment or seem unduly personal, but how different is this from talking to a gynecologist?

By nature, we women grit our teeth when we have to visit a gynecologist, but we go. We realize that our physical health is at stake and that the gynecologist is a professional, whose intention is to help. Consequently, we overcome whatever embarrassment we feel when talking to him.

The same should apply to an even greater extent when talking to a Rav. He is dedicated to our spiritual well-being, and his questions are asked with the sole purpose of verifying facts in order to be of service to us.

The thought that a learned scholar, trained in the service of God and anxious to help his fellowmen, is willing to give us his time and attention should be a source of reassurance and satisfaction. Thus, there is no place for hesitation or shame in asking the Rav any questions. Rather, we should be matter-of-fact in our approach, providing all the information needed.

There is a further point necessary to remember in this context. A Rav is trained to assist a woman in maintaining a state of *taharah* and not to declare her a *niddah* unless it is absolutely necessary. There is a need for strict and careful adherence to the *niddah* laws, but there is no need for stringencies that go beyond those required by the Torah.

A woman's state of *niddah* is at times an unavoidable reality of life. However, the *niddah* state does have its own specific advantages. It protects a woman physically and emotionally and gives her time for self-rejuvenation and an opportunity for spiritual growth, as we have discussed.

Nevertheless, when at all possible, the Torah is anxious for a woman to be regarded as *tehorah* and, thus, have access to the abundance of physical and spiritual well-being that the state of *taharah* brings.

A Rav is trained to know when stringency is required and when it is out of place. We must rely on his judgement and realize that he is trying to arrive at a halachic decision that is in our own best interests and in harmony with the workings of our bodies. A proper attitude on our part can greatly assist him in guiding us.

Consulting a Rav is Both a Requirement and an Advantage

1. Only a Rav can determine the status of spots and stains of a questionable type, size, or coloring.

2. A Rav can be helpful when problems arise which are related to difficulties in becoming pregnant.

3. A Rav can advise a woman who has difficulty in making *bedikot*, internal checks.

4. A Rav can provide superb Torah-oriented counseling in cases of marital difficulties.

5. Refraining from consulting a Rav is not considered an act of modesty. Quite the contrary, one must never be too embarrassed to approach a Rav.

6. When consulting a Rav, a woman should state her question clearly, providing all the necessary information.

Typical Information to Keep in Mind When Consulting a Rav

What day of her cycle did the woman discover the discharge? Was she *tehorah*? Was it the day she was expecting her period? Was the discharge found after the *hefsek taharah* (see chap. 5)? Was it on a *bedikah* cloth? Was it on the *moch dachuk* (see chap. 5)? What was its size? Were any of the following conditions involved: pregnancy, nursing, childbirth, a gynecologist's examination, gynecological problems, fertility problems? Does the question regard a *bedikah* cloth? Was it checked to verify cleanliness before use? Does the question regard a garment? What is the color and type of material (synthetic or natural)? Did she sense a discharge of fluid from the vagina? Is she a bride prior to her wedding or newly married? Was the staining found after intercourse? After urinating? How soon after? Does she have a hemorrhoid problem?

Whenever a question arises which may render a woman a *niddah*, she must refrain from physical contact with her husband until she receives the Rav's decision. Needless to say, she should never regard a question lightly and consider herself *tehorah* without proper halachic determination. However, neither should she go to the other extreme and consider herself a *niddah* in order to save herself the inconvenience of consulting with a Rav.

Rabbi Abrams was studying with a colleague when a brightly colored convertible pulled up to his door. A woman who was clearly a stranger emerged slowly from the car and proceeded towards the doorway with an envelope in her hand. She hesitated a moment and then rang the bell. Rabbi Abrams answered the door and with a smile invited the woman into his home. With a trace of embarrassment, she extended the envelope to the Rabbi. In it was a *bedikah* cloth, and on it were written the details of the internal inspection.

"Is it okay?" the woman asked. "I don't know much about religious law, but the counselor who taught me these laws emphasized the necessity of bringing questionable colors to a Rav—and it's so important to me to do everything 100%."

CHAPTER 4

The Spotless Week

THE HIGH PRIEST in the Holy Temple was garbed in splendid clothing. Multicolored threads, hand woven into a magnificent garment, and ornamental bells adorning his robe underscored the unique position which he occupied in the service of God.

When the High Priest entered the Holy Temple, the ringing of the bells about his robe would announce his arrival. Our Sages drew a parallel from the behavior of the High Priest in the Temple to that of every man in his "miniature sanctuary"—his own private home. "Do not enter your home suddenly," they counseled. "Every husband should emulate the High Priest's example and make others aware of his presence before entering his home."

Indeed, this idea is as valid for a woman as it is for a man. As a woman begins married life and commits herself to

God's divine plan for Jewish living, *Taharat HaMishpachah*, she must not "enter suddenly." One cannot simply burst into this lifestyle without proper preparation.

Before and after the marriage ceremony, it is our privilege and obligation to study and learn the detailed laws of *Taharat HaMishpachah*. We as women are aware of the many different facets, functions, moods, and capabilities that are so characteristic of our femininity. The detailed laws of *Taharat HaMishpachah* reflect our many-sided nature. Through the study of these laws, we learn to understand ourselves better and gain greater awareness of the plan God designed for married life.

An electrician was called upon to install the electricity in a new building. He arrived promptly and set to work on the wires. After working for a short time connecting wires here and putting in switches there, he announced that his work was completed.

"But surely you couldn't have finished the job so quickly!" exclaimed the customer. "I'm not very familiar with this wiring, but I do believe you did your job in record time."

"Sure," replied the electrician with confidence. "I'm an expert. I know what I'm doing." However, his pleasure was short-lived, and his smile turned to a frown when he tried to switch on the unit. It didn't work!

"What do you say to this?" demanded the customer.

The electrician shrugged. "Sorry to disappoint you, sir. Look, I did connect the main wires. As for some of the small wires—well, you see, I'm just not a fanatic for details."

We must approach *Taharat HaMishpachah* earnestly. "Getting the general idea" or "doing what I understand" is not sufficient. When a tiny wire is disconnected, an entire electrical unit will not function. Similarly, if a woman ignores even a seemingly slight aspect of the laws of *Taharat Ha-Mishpachah*, she may completely invalidate all the practices she has taken upon herself.

Taharat HaMishpachah should bring us happiness, satisfaction, and inner peace. However, by no means should the comfort and relaxation we feel in its observance give way to casualness or carelessness.

A woman who constantly seeks stringencies, overzealously clinging to her conception of the laws, and one who keeps the laws carelessly, ignoring basic elements of their performance, share the same fundamental error: neither is committed to following the mitzvah as it is. Both allow their own conception (or misconception) of what *Taharat Ha-Mishpachah* is to control their behavior.

Neither extreme is correct. We must commit ourselves to the study and review of these laws so that we understand them in their totality and are able to fulfill them as God desires.

Lacking the knowledge of fine details can also be the cause of much unnecessary discomfort and hardship.

Miriam was a young newlywed. She felt a sense of growth and development as she confronted the challenges of married life. She felt confident and happy, ready and eager, to create a pleasant atmosphere in her meticulously kept home.

She found herself, however, in a difficult predicament. Here she was, six weeks after her wedding, and she was still unable to go to the *mikvah* again. Miriam had studied the laws of *Taharat HaMishpachah* prior to her marriage. Based on what she had learned, she could not recall any chapter that dealt with a situation similar to hers.

Miriam was making one small yet crucial mistake. She was trying to "go it alone." She had studied with a competent *Taharat HaMishpachah* counselor. She understood and was willing to accept the laws. Only one thing bothered her—going to a Rav. What the counselor said on this subject went in one ear and out the other. She was determined that no Rav would ever see her underwear!

Desperately, she turned to a friend for guidance. The friend introduced Miriam to a more experienced *Taharat HaMishpachah* counselor. In a patient manner, the woman discussed the issues with Miriam and convinced her to make an appointment with a Rav.

Miriam was very embarrassed afterwards. The Rav informed her that she hadn't been a *niddah* and could have gone to the *mikvah*. All the aggravation she and her husband had gone through was for nothing!

But not entirely for nothing. Call it "learning the hard way," if you will. Miriam finally understood that she ought not to rely on her own judgement, but should call a Rav when a problem arises.

Miriam is not alone. Many women who are committed to the practice of *Taharat HaMishpachah* are unaware of the detailed aspects of the laws. Therefore, it is advisable for a woman to find a Rav (or *Taharat HaMishpachah* counselor) with whom she feels comfortable discussing any questions which may arise.

Indeed, after a woman marries, it is advisable for her to periodically review the laws of *Taharat HaMishpachah*. Because of the detailed nature of these laws, we are likely to forget or overlook certain aspects of them as time passes. Also, when a woman is pregnant or exclusively nursing, she generally does not enter the state of *niddah*. These long intervals, in which the laws are not put into practice, may lead to forgetting many particulars.

Among the other reasons for continued review of these laws are:

1. *Taharat HaMishpachah* is a private and intimate topic. When the laws and concepts were first presented, we may have shied away from asking questions to clarify points that seemed unclear. As we become more familiar and comfortable with the laws, we may find it easier to communicate our questions and observations.

2. These laws were taught to us before marriage, when we lacked the opportunity to observe the practical application of many of these concepts. As we gain more experience in observing *Taharat HaMishpachah*, a review may prove very helpful, for we will now have firsthand knowledge of what were before only theoretical terms.

3. A bride-to-be is very preoccupied with wedding preparations and the redefinition of her personality which marriage entails. Frequently, by the time she sits down to study with a *Taharat HaMishpachah* counselor, she is emotionally and physically drained. This is obviously not the ideal state of mind to be in to fully comprehend complex laws!

4. In previous generations, a mother would teach the observance of *Taharat HaMishpachah* to her daughter in a

direct, personal, and loving way. In contrast, many women today acquire familiarity with the subject only through classes, books, and lectures. None of these methods is as satisfactory as the personal approach.

There is no way we can totally compensate for the loss of the unique opportunity of a mother-daughter teaching situation. However, the awareness that our knowledge of the subject is lacking this dimension should motivate us to try to supplement it in whatever way possible. Learning individually with a *Taharat HaMishpachah* counselor is the only method which can compare to the mother-daughter arrangement of previous generations.

5.   In different communities, there are certain practices that are connected with the laws of *Taharat HaMishpachah.* Many misconceptions can arise out of the confusion of these practices with Torah and Rabbinic law, so a clear distinction must be made. Adequate review will allow a woman to distinguish between those practices which are absolute requirements and those which are not required by law.

Sarah had been married for seven years. Both she and her husband desperately desired children. As a consequence, her failure to become pregnant had made her extremely anxious.

She mentioned to a friend that she was constantly nervous and, perhaps, overly stringent in her observance of *Taharat HaMishpachah.* When an appropriate opportunity presented itself, her friend suggested that Sarah join a study group for review of the laws.

"Who me?" Sarah retorted with a touch of bitterness in her voice.

"I'm so careful and particular with the laws. Besides, pregnancy and nursing haven't interrupted my monthly visits to the *mikvah*. I'm an expert by now!"

Nevertheless, after some gentle coaxing, she agreed to attend the class. Much to her amazement, Sarah discovered that her self-imposed, stringent manner of observance was not in accordance with the law.

With the counselor's encouragement, Sarah resolved to increase her knowledge of the laws and find out what she was supposed to do. She consulted a Rav for guidance and followed his instructions. The more she learned, the more she became aware of how wrong she had been.

Within a year, a very happy Sarah gave birth to a healthy daughter. She called the baby Kaila after her late grandmother. The first Shabbat the new family spent together at home, Sarah's husband observed with a grin, "There may be more to the baby's name than we realized. The name 'Kaila' resembles the Hebrew word *kal*, which means 'easy.' *Mitzvot* are 'easy' when observed correctly in accordance with the law."

The stress on detailed study certainly does not mean that a woman should try to become a Rav. Through her study, however, she can and should obtain an awareness of which information is important to a Rav and what factors will be helpful to him in his decision-making process. Often, the knowledge of these factors can make a world of difference.

Mrs. Blau is a professional marriage counselor. She is also an experienced teacher of *Taharat HaMishpachah.*

Here is her own account of a situation in which lack of knowledge of details caused one bride to be unnecessarily anxious.

"It was a pleasant evening in May. My husband and I were driving out to the suburbs to join some friends for their housewarming celebration.

"As we passed through the city, my husband suddenly exclaimed, 'Oh! I almost forgot. Tonight is the wedding of the son of one of my business acquaintances. I didn't really plan on going, but since it's not out of our way, let's stop in just to wish them *mazel tov!*'

"I felt a little awkward entering the wedding hall. I didn't know anyone there. Or at least I thought I didn't.

"Much to my surprise, a woman whose face looked familiar literally ran up to me. I recognized her as a new *Taharat HaMishpachah* counselor whom I had met at a teachers' convention.

"'Mrs. Blau,' she called. 'You cannot imagine how happy I am to see you here. I didn't know you were invited, but, never mind, you have arrived as if God sent you.'

"I could not imagine what this was all about, but she didn't keep me wondering for long. 'You see,' the counselor continued worriedly, 'the bride just discovered a stain that renders her a *niddah!* Can you imagine? Right before the *chupah!*'

"'I've become very close to her during our sessions, and sh. '. .gged me to properly organize the procedure for tonight. I know there are arrangements to be made, but how do I explain them? Please help me. This has never happened to me before, and though I know the laws involved, I could use your assistance.'

"The entire situation came upon me so unexpectedly. I reviewed the proper steps to be taken in such a case and imagined the unavoidable discomfort. If the bride is a *niddah*, the groom cannot touch her. They cannot spend the night as man and wife. As I was pondering over the issue, I instinctively asked the counselor what circumstances had rendered the bride a *niddah*.

"As soon as the question left my lips, I regretted it. Who was I to doubt the counselor? Wouldn't she feel slighted? But my experience with overlooked details dictated that I ask. I inquired further as to the manner in which the question was presented to the Rav who had decided that the bride was a *niddah*.

"The counselor was only too eager for my involvement, and we discussed the matter in detail. I quickly realized that the question had not been posed properly; were the Rav to be given a corrected version, with important details that had been omitted, a different decision might be made.

"Sure enough, when the question was rephrased and the bride herself spoke to the Rav, mentioning additional details, the Rav changed his decision: The *niddah* bride was not a *niddah*. After all this, how could I not share in the joy of this bride and groom even though I didn't know them? As we continued our drive to our original destination, I found myself saying out loud: 'Thank God for details....'

"My husband gave me a quizzical glance, but I merely shrugged. 'Oh, it's not important. It's just that, at times, what you don't know can hurt you.'"

The very fact that the laws are so detailed and multi-faceted can often convince a person of their extreme importance.

Sharon is a woman in her late thirties who has been keeping *Taharat HaMishpachah* for sixteen years. Her observance would not seem at all noteworthy if it were not for the fact that, for much of that time, her husband took no interest whatsoever in these practices.

"I love you, and I sense we have a special marriage, so I'm willing to go along with it," he would frequently tell his wife. "But that's it. I'm not interested in learning and understanding these laws. I'll do whatever you want, but after a full day's work, there are other things to which I want to devote whatever mental energy I have left."

Sharon persisted stubbornly. She was convinced that her husband's becoming aware of the reasons behind *Taharat HaMishpachah* would add a deeper dimension to her marriage. She coaxed and pleaded, but to no avail.

One day, it occurred to her to organize a study group on the subject in her home and schedule the meetings at the times when her husband was home. Sharon casually told her husband about the weekly class to be held in their living room and requested that he make himself comfortable in the adjoining study, as it was mainly "a topic of interest to women."

That very description aroused his curiosity. The class began the next week with a sizeable attendance. Unbeknownst to the teacher, an additional "student" was listening attentively behind the study door.

The sessions continued weekly, with the teacher explaining the issues in depth and answering a multitude of questions. Sharon's husband was fascinated by what he heard, and he was extremely impressed by how the laws accommodated all levels of human functioning.

"There is a unique blend of universality and personal relevance to these laws," he mused to himself. "On the one hand, they revolve around unchanging, objective principles, yet they also appear to be tailor-made for every individual, down to the most minute detail."

Sharon sensed the change that was coming over her husband and was only too happy to encourage it. She continues to reap the benefits of her cunning scheme to this day. When she meets friends who are confronting a similar situation—uninvolved husbands—she shares her secret with them (and the advantage of having a study adjoining the living room).

The transition from *niddah* to *taharah*, and the laws which govern this transition, is a fundamental component of the system of *Taharat HaMishpachah*. A woman who has entered the state of *niddah* follows a procedure of separation, preparation, and sanctification. While a woman is a *niddah*, she and her husband refrain from physical contact. As will be explained in chapter six, this allows them the opportunity to express their love and devotion to each other in other ways.

While our husbands are patiently waiting, we are actively preparing ourselves for the time of our physical reunion. The cumulative effect of all the procedures we perform to insure our readiness is to make us more aware of our bodies.

Inspections of the vagina, using a white cotton cloth to insure maximum comfort and efficiency, are at the center of our preparations. These internal checks are carried out throughout the entire seven spotless day period, right up to the time of our immersion in the *mikvah*. The laws explaining this procedure will be discussed in the following chapter.

These inspections are termed *bedikot*. The cloth we use is called the *bedikah* cloth, or *ayd*. The literal translation of *ayd* is "witness," for it serves as "evidence" of our readiness to resume marital relations. The purpose of the *bedikot* is to detect any possibility of continued bleeding or staining from the uterus that might render a woman a *niddah*.

The *bedikot* help us "know" our bodies and be aware of our womanly functions. This self-knowledge has, in fact, characterized and distinguished Jewish women throughout the ages. The first chapter of *Shemot* relates how Pharaoh commanded the Jewish midwives to slay all male children.

The midwives failed to comply with this order. They explained that Jewish women were *chayot*—alive with themselves, in touch with their bodies. They would give birth on their own without waiting for the midwife to arrive. Once a child was born, the midwives were unable to take it from its mother.

Taharat HaMishpachah gives us a unique opportunity to serve God with our very bodies. Women, like men, are obliged to keep the Torah's commandments. Unlike men, however, they are exempt from fulfilling those positive commandments which involve a time factor.

There are 248 positive commandments. The Hebrew numerical value for that number is *ramach*—the letters *reish*, *mem*, and *chet*. The Hebrew word for uterus is *rechem*—again, the letters *reish*, *chet*, and *mem*. Thus, we see that our very femininity encompasses and, in some way, allows for the fulfillment of all the positive commandments—even those from which we are exempt.

Our performing the *bedikot* further expresses that which is unique in our service of God, because the *bedikot* show how the *mitzvot* can and should involve that which is most corporeal about ourselves.

Nevertheless, this all-encompassing approach requires a careful observance of the laws. If the *hefsek taharah* is not carried out in the proper manner, a woman remains a *niddah;* she cannot immerse herself in the *mikvah* even if she continued counting the seven spotless days afterwards. Think of the repercussions carelessness or lack of knowledge in this matter can bring!

Mrs. Cohen had been a *Taharat HaMishpachah* counselor for eight years. She had lectured frequently on the subject and had an easygoing but thorough approach to teaching the laws. Once, in the middle of a study session on how to make a *hefsek taharah,* her presentation was interrupted rather rudely.

"That's nonsense," shouted Mrs. Lefkowitz. "I've been making a *hefsek taharah* for fifteen years. I have five children. I wasn't taught to do it that way."

The other women were shocked. They all knew Mrs. Lefkowitz as an observant woman. Maybe...

Mrs. Cohen didn't leave them much time to ponder the question. Tactfully, but firmly, she replied: "I respect your practices, but what I am teaching is 100 percent correct. So I'll teach it this way, and after the lesson, you and I will get together and compare notes."

After the class, Mrs. Lefkowitz sought out Mrs. Cohen. "I didn't want to interrupt you again," she ventured, "but I still say you're wrong. Here's how I do a *hefsek*."

As Mrs. Cohen heard her description, she felt herself in a very delicate situation. How could she tell this woman who was so sure she was right that she was making a crucial mistake. "You know," she replied, "there are real differences between what you're saying and what I teach. Look, tomorrow morning, I have an appointment with Rav Weinstein. Come with me, and we'll ask him to clarify the matter once and for all."

Mrs. Lefkowitz was willing. She respected Rav Weinstein very much. She "knew" that he would verify her description of what to do.

After a ten minute discussion, Rav Weinstein asked Mrs. Cohen to postpone their meeting. She left while he continued speaking with Mrs. Lefkowitz, who finally emerged from the Rav's office in tears. For fifteen years, she had not been doing a *hefsek taharah* correctly.

Unfortunately, mistakes of this nature are far too common. One *Taharat HaMishpachah* counselor recounts meeting a woman who told her how she had carried out every aspect of the *Taharat HaMishpachah* laws properly for twelve years. The counselor listened and saw that the woman was making a fundamental mistake. She had counted the *hefsek taharah* as the first of the seven clean days. This means that she had never gone to the *mikvah* on the right day. For twelve years, she had remained a *niddah*.

The *bedikot* can prove beneficial medically, as well. After menstruation, the uterus needs a certain amount of time to renew its inner lining. The *bedikot* will immediately detect if there is anything amiss. Often, a *bedikah* can uncover a health problem even before physical discomfort would lead us to a doctor's office for examination.

Vera was a young woman of twenty-six, a mother of three children and actively involved in many community affairs. A bundle of energy, she expressed her abilities and skills in many ways. The furthest thought from her mind was illness....

Taharat HaMishpachah was her way of life, and she observed all its aspects with commitment and joy. During one menstrual cycle, as she was preparing to make the transition from the *niddah* to the *taharah* state, she detected continuous staining on the *bedikot* long after it usually stopped. She didn't experience heavy bleeding and would have dismissed it as an internal sore.

However, since the stains prevented her from continuing the process of preparation for immersion in the *mikvah,* she consulted a Rav. He thought the problem unusual and suggested a doctor's examination.

It was with mixed feelings that Vera scheduled an appointment. Although she knew it was the right thing to do, she felt that she couldn't be bothered with doctors. If not for the dictates of the laws of *Taharat HaMishpachah,* she probably would have ignored the whole situation. "As a matter of fact," she explained later, "if not for the *bedikot,* I would never have detected the staining."

In fact, those *bedikot* may have saved her life. The doctor's examination revealed a tumor, which was, thank God, removed. Today, Vera is back to her busy life and grateful for every day of health.

She often quotes the doctor who treated her. "You're a very lucky lady, Vera. The tumor was discovered while it was in its early stages. We were able to remove it relatively easily and are reasonably sure that it will not reoccur. I wonder what made you come in for a checkup? It seemed as though you almost knew something was wrong. But in that stage, how could you have known?..."

If we dedicate ourselves to keeping these laws and study them thoroughly, God will grant us the ability to fulfill them as He intended. "Sanctify yourselves, and you will be holy" (VaYikra 20:7). Our Sages comment on this verse: "If a person makes the effort to sanctify himself even slightly, God will make him holy both in this world and the world to come" (Yoma 39). The Vilna Gaon explains that holiness does not descend from heaven; rather, man himself, through his actions, brings about holiness.

CHAPTER 5

The Countdown

What Is a *Hefsek Taharah*?

AFTER A WOMAN'S menstrual bleeding has ceased, she must inspect herself to confirm her readiness for the preparation that leads to the change of status from *niddah* to *taharah*.

The *hefsek taharah*, the confirmation of the end of menstrual bleeding, involves an internal inspection of the vagina to check that bleeding from the uterus has entirely ceased. Once a woman has verified this, she may begin counting the *shiva niki'im*, the seven spotless days, from the following day. The day on which the *hefsek taharah* is carried out is not counted as one of the seven spotless days.

When Can a Woman Perform the *Hefsek Taharah?*

A woman cannot make a *hefsek taharah* until the afternoon of the fifth day after she has entered the state of *niddah*. The day on which her period began is counted as the first of these five days. For this reason, and also to help calculate *onot* (see chap. 10), it is advisable to mark down on a personal calendar the Hebrew date when menstruation began, and whether it began in the daytime or at night, i.e., before or after *shkiyah*, sunset.

The Hebrew calendar date is from sunset to sunset. For example: If a woman's period began after sunset on Tuesday or any time on Wednesday till sunset, she cannot make the *hefsek taharah bedikah* until Sunday before sunset.

A woman must wait five days, even if her menstruation ceases before that time. Obviously, a woman with a longer period must wait until she is able to perform the *hefsek taharah.**

These five days are required when immediately prior to the onset of menstruation, the woman had been *tehorah*, i.e., not a *niddah*. However, a woman who had already been a *niddah* for five days—for example, because of a stain that was judged as blood—and then her menstrual period commenced, may carry out a *hefsek taharah* as soon as possible.

---

*A woman past menopause, or in the midst of pregnancy, who only then becomes aware of *Taharat HaMishpachah* and commits herself to this lifestyle must also observe this practice. She, too, must abstain from physical contact with her husband and count five days prior to making the *hefsek taharah bedikah*. Afterwards, she, as all other women, must count seven spotless days before immersing in the *mikvah*.

For example: A woman discovers a stain rendering her *niddah* on Sunday. She waits five days, but on Thursday she begins menstruating. Since five days have already passed in the state of *niddah*, she does not have to wait an additional five days from Thursday. If she has a shorter menstrual period, she may make the *hefsek taharah bedikah* as soon as she is able.

The same applies to a woman who discovers a stain, which is determined to be blood, during her seven spotless days. She may perform another *hefsek taharah* as soon as she can.

Specific Leniencies

1. A bride-to-be does not have to wait five days after menstruation when preparing herself for her initial immersion. Rather, she is allowed to carry out the *hefsek taharah* as soon as possible.*

2. A newlywed bride who becomes a *niddah* due to hymenal bleeding may carry out a *hefsek taharah* four days after becoming a *niddah* if she is able.

3. Women who are ovulating before immersing in the *mikvah* and, consequently, are having difficulty becoming pregnant, should consult a Rav. He is trained to offer a number of possible solutions to the problem.

---

*This leniency does not apply to a bride who was unfamiliar with Jewish Law prior to her wedding and who was not abstaining from physical relations with her groom. They must abstain from physical contact five days before she does the *hefsek taharah*.

4. A woman who discovers blood after her immersion in the *mikvah* and before resuming marital relations need not wait for five days and may make a *hefsek taharah* immediately. However, because of the unusual nature of this instance, it is advisable to consult a Rav.

What Is the Right Time of Day for the *Hefsek Taharah Bedikah?*

The *hefsek taharah bedikah* must be made before sunset. The proper time is between a half-hour to one hour beforehand. If that time is inconvenient, the procedure may be carried out up to two hours prior to sunset.

(As long as the *bedikah* is carried out before sunset, it is acceptable. However, it is advisable to begin some time beforehand so that there will not be a nervous race against the clock. Also, should blood be discovered during the initial attempt at carrying out a *bedikah,* further attempts will be possible if sufficient time is available.)

In cases of extreme difficulty (e.g., the woman will be traveling on a bus without comfortable facilities during that entire time) a woman should consult a Rav. (There are leniencies, but it is necessary to follow authoritative instructions.)

What Is the Procedure for the *Hefsek Taharah?*

1. Washing

2. The *bedikah*—internal inspection with a *bedikah* cloth

Washing

A woman should wash the lower half of her body or at least the genital area and inside the vagina with water (warm water is suggested for her comfort). This washing is for her benefit. It is intended to rinse out tiny spots of blood or residue and help her avoid discovering stains in the following days. When it is impossible to wash, it is enough for a woman to wipe herself internally instead.

On Shabbat and Yom Kippur, the procedure is changed slightly because of the Shabbat laws. On Shabbat, a woman should use cold water or water which has been heated before Shabbat. Furthermore, she should not use a sponge or wet cloth. On Yom Kippur, Tishah B'av, or during the week of her *shiva* mourning period, when washing for pleasure is prohibited, she may wash, but only the minimum area necessary.

It is advisable to wait ten to fifteen minutes after washing before making the *bedikah*. By doing so, any excess water will drain, and the vagina's natural lubrication will return. This will ease the performing of the *bedikah*. If there is not sufficient time to wait these fifteen minutes, a woman should wipe the inside of her vagina dry before making the *bedikah*.*

*It is unnecessary and inadvisable to use a "douche" for this washing procedure. Should a woman insist on doing so, she *must* wait at least fifteen minutes before making the *bedikah*.

The *Bedikah*

What Should Be Used for a *Bedikah* Cloth?

The *bedikah* cloth, which should be checked prior to use, should be absolutely clean, soft, white, absorbent, and made from a nonsynthetic fabric. Cotton cloths are generally used. It is not permitted to use a tampon. It is not advisable to use cotton wool (cotton balls) since its strands separate. Do not use a handkerchief because it may cause sores.

The cloth should be between two-and-one-half to three inches square (six to eight centimeters square). Packages of cloths meeting these requirements can usually be obtained at a local *mikvah*.

How Is the Internal Inspection Performed?

Wrap the cloth around the index finger. Be careful with long fingernails, because they may cause scratching. A suggested position for maximum comfort and efficiency is to lift one leg up on a chair.

Insert the finger, the cloth wrapped around it, into the vagina as deep as possible. The entire finger should be inserted. Slowly and gently, rotate the finger inside the vagina to check all folds and clefts. Continue rotating the finger, as you direct it from deep inside back out while gently pressing on the vaginal canal.

The rotating motion is intended to detect any drop of blood that may be left in the many folds of the vaginal lining. Rotating with a soft cloth is most efficient. A tampon, by contrast, does not reach the crevices.

If a woman finds difficulty in carrying out the *bedikah* due to lack of natural lubrication, she may wet the cloth and then squeeze it out entirely before performing the *bedikah*. If she still has a problem, she should consult a Rav. Needless to say, a virgin bride should be careful to insert her finger only as far as is comfortable when performing this *bedikah* so as to avoid discomfort or bleeding.

It must be emphasized that this internal inspection is not merely a stringency but, rather, an absolute requirement for making a *hefsek taharah*. A woman who merely wipes herself externally has not fulfilled the law and cannot continue the *taharah* process until she performs this internal examination as prescribed.

What to Look for on the *Bedikah* Cloth *(Ayd)* after the Internal Inspection

Check the cloth by daylight (but not directly in the sun). It should be clean and free of any stains. It may be helpful for a woman wearing glasses to remove them. If there is not enough light to check the cloth, place it in a clean place where it will not be lost and inspect it by daylight on the following day.

If red stains are found on this *bedikah* cloth, one may wash again and carry out another inspection (with a different cloth) until a clean *bedikah* is obtained. Obviously, this additional examination must be performed before sunset. A woman performing additional *bedikot* should do so gently and carefully in order to prevent any irritation or discomfort.

If questionable stains are found on the cloth used for the last examination before sunset, the cloth should be put in an envelope, preferably after it is dry, to be taken later to a Rav. Nevertheless, the woman should continue with the *taharah* process until the Rav's decision is made.

The *Moch Dochuk*

A widely-practiced custom, and one which must be adopted by *every* woman unless instructed otherwise by her Rav, is the use of a *moch dochuk*.

What to Do

After a clean *bedikah* has been made, insert another *bedikah* cloth (called a *moch dochuk*) into the vaginal canal and leave it there from before sunset until the emergence of three stars. At that time, the cloth should be removed and checked for any stains. It should be kept overnight in an envelope in a place where it will not be lost and rechecked again by daylight the next morning.

Regular *bedikah* cloths with a string attached specifically for this purpose can be obtained at most *mikvaot*. If a woman does not have any other *bedikah* cloths, the cloth she used for the *hefsek taharah* may be used for the *moch* if it has first been thoroughly checked and found clean.

The purpose of the *moch dochuk* is to detect any bleeding which may occur at the end of the day. The halacha considers this as a time of transition when verification is fundamentally important. Also, due to the woman's washing, bleeding may have stopped momentarily, only to be resumed a short while later. The *moch* will detect this.

Suggestions Regarding *Moch Dochuk*

1. Lie down if it is uncomfortable to walk around while the *moch* is in place.

2. If there was a question regarding the *hefsek taharah bedikah*, rotate the *moch* so it may also serve as a *hefsek taharah bedikah* if necessary.

3. It is not advisable to use a tampon as a *moch*, as it penetrates too deeply. Also, it cannot be checked as easily as a cloth.

4. Consult a Rav if inserting a *moch* causes vaginal irritation and staining. (This may occur after childbirth.)

Additional Points

If the *hefsek taharah* or the *moch dochuk* inspections prove to be halachically unacceptable (e.g., stains, improper procedure, or inappropriate timing, etc.), the process should be attempted again on the following day before sunset.

Totally clean white underwear should be worn after the *hefsek taharah bedikah* and for the duration of the seven spotless days.

It is advisable for a woman to note the day she completed a halachically acceptable *hefsek taharah* on her personal calendar. Having such a calendar can help prevent mistakes.

The Seven Spotless Days—*Shiva Niki'im*

Ruth lived in Eretz Yisrael. She and her family had come to spend the Pesach holidays with her parents in New York. She had left Eretz Yisrael in the middle of counting the seven spotless days. She didn't give the matter a second thought. There are *mikvaot* all over the world. On the contrary, she heard that the local *mikvah* near her parents had been renovated and modernized and was interested to see the new facilities.

When packing, Ruth questioned whether to take her personal calendar. "No," she thought. "We're only going for two weeks. I'm already past the *hefsek*. What for?"

The trip was more tiring than usual. Ruth's baby kept her up most of the time. Both she and the baby were jet-lagged for a number of days afterwards. Time became a little fuzzy.

To make a long story short, Ruth ended up visiting the renovated *mikvah* twice. The first time as she was emerging from the water after immersion, she felt queer. Something was wrong. Nervously, she dressed and checked the calendar on the *mikvah* door, trying to remember. After a few moments, she recalled: This was the sixth and not the seventh day after the *hefsek*. She had immersed while still a *niddah*.

With slight embarrassment, but happy to be able to keep the laws correctly, she returned to immerse the following night.

From the day after the *hefsek taharah*, a woman must count seven consecutive spotless days before immersing herself in the *mikvah*. She must inspect herself internally twice on each of these days, once in the morning and once before sunset, to make sure that there is no sign of uterine bleeding.

How to Count

The seven days must be continuous and complete. For example: a woman making her *hefsek taharah* on Thursday before sunset begins her seven spotless days on Friday. She will immerse in the *mikvah* on the following Thursday night.

The obligation to count these seven days stems from the verse: "And she shall count for herself " (*VaYikra* 15:29). The verse implies that a woman should consciously count the days, saying to herself: "Today is day one," "Today, day two," etc.

The Torah regards a woman's intention and awareness as an integral part of the observance of this mitzvah. Thus, questions may arise if a woman makes a mental decision to interrupt her counting. Take the example of a woman who finds a stain which appears to her as blood and who, before receiving clarification from a Rav as to her status, considers the stain impure and pays no further attention to her previous counting. Subsequently, the stain is shown to a Rav who decides that it is not problematic. This woman cannot simply take up her counting where she left off. Rather, she must consult a Rav.

Alternatively, a woman interrupts her count of seven spotless days because her husband intends to be out of town at the time of her scheduled immersion. His schedule changes, and, consequently, the woman is eager to resume her original count. She, too, must consult a Rav.

In all such instances, a Rav must be consulted to verify whether it is necessary to begin a new reckoning of the seven spotless days. Because of this question, it is desirable to avoid the entire issue and never interrupt the original counting. Thus, a woman who consults a Rav with a question regarding a stain should continue her counting while awaiting his answer.*

If a woman completes the seven-day reckoning and must, because of a sound halachic reason, postpone her immersion, her counting is still valid. However, white underwear and sheet need not be used for longer than the seven days.

What Must a Woman Do during the Seven Spotless Days?

1. The two bedikot, one in the morning and one before sunset, are performed in the same manner as explained above regarding the hefsek taharah bedikah—insert the bedikah cloth deeply and rotate.

2. The vaginal area should not be washed before making the bedikah.

3. The moch dochuk procedure is not performed.

4. Women should wear white underwear which should be checked every day.

---

*A situation may arise where the Rav's decision is delayed so that the woman does not know if she needs to start the count anew with a new hefsek taharah or she should simply continue the seven-day count. In such a case, she may perform a new hefsek taharah "on condition," i.e., if the Rav's decision will be that she has to start the count anew, she has already done a new hefsek taharah. In this way, no days will be lost.

5. Throughout the ages, women have adopted the custom of sleeping on a white sheet which should be checked every day during these seven days.

Stains Found on a *Bedikah* Cloth or Other Stains (on the Body or Clothes) Discovered during These Seven Days

Consult a Rav and inform him:

1. when the *hefsek taharah bedikah* was done;

2. on which of the seven days the stain was found.

If the Rav decides that such a stain is a problematic one, the woman must perform a new *hefsek taharah* (including the *moch dochuk* procedure) as soon as she can and begin counting anew. In this instance, she need not wait five days before performing the *hefsek taharah* since such an interval had already passed before she began her first seven-day count.

What If the *Bedikot* Were Not Carried Out?

If a woman was unable (not merely neglectful) or forgot to make *bedikot*, some leniency does apply. The basic rule is: A *bedikah* is imperative on the *first* and *seventh* days after the *hefsek taharah*. If the *bedikot* were not carried out on any of the intermediate days, this does not invalidate a woman's seven-day count. Nevertheless, a woman must seriously attempt to do all fourteen *bedikot*. In all cases of missed *bedikot*, it is preferable to consult a Rav.

Suggestions and Advice

1. Make the morning *bedikah* immediately upon rising so as not to forget.

2. If leaving home in the afternoon, carry a packet of *bedikah* cloths in your purse, just in case you're prevented from getting home before sunset.

3. Consult a Rav if the *bedikot* cause discomfort of any sort.

4. Do not bathe immediately prior to doing a *bedikah*.

CHAPTER 6

Making the Heart Grow Fonder

RABBI ARYEH LEVIN, of blessed memory, was a renowned figure in Jerusalem. Those who knew him said that his entire being radiated true love and selfless concern for his fellow Jew.

Once, Reb Aryeh accompanied his wife on a visit to the doctor. They sat patiently in the corridor, awaiting their appointment. When the nurse called Rebbetzin Levin in, she was surprised to see Reb Aryeh get up as well.

The doctor, too, was surprised when the couple entered his office together. Surely this woman was capable of consulting a physician on her own. But he was soon provided with an explanation. Reb Aryeh sat his wife comfortably in a chair and, turning to the doctor, said:

"Good morning, sir. We've come to seek your professional advice. You see, my wife's leg hurts us...."

The Torah wishes us to develop such empathetic marriages. But how can such a bond be established? And how can we preserve that bond over an entire lifetime? Human nature tends to tire of familiar situations. Indeed, one of the major factors behind today's skyrocketing divorce figures is downright boredom. A husband and wife simply lose interest in each other, complaining that the other has nothing more to offer.

This is not solely a modern-day phenomenon. Thousands of years ago, the Torah recognized the problem and offered our people a basic guideline on how to overcome it:

Rabbi Meir said: "Why did the Torah require a niddah to be impure for seven days? because her husband could become bored with her and tire of her. Therefore, the Torah declares, 'Let her be ritually impure for seven days so that she will be as dear to her husband as when she entered the marriage canopy.'"

(Tractate Niddah 31b)

While a woman is a *niddah*, she and her husband abstain from physical contact, and, to paraphrase a popular expression, *abstinence makes the heart grow fonder.* The rules of the *harchakot*, maintaining a distance, are the framework in which a husband and wife practice their abstinence and through which it is hoped they will develop an even closer connection.

Many psychologists and marriage counselors adopt a similar approach when guiding a couple who are undergoing difficulties in their relationship. They suggest the parties avoid physical contact for a set time in the hope that this separation will rekindle their attraction for one another.

There is, however, an obvious advantage when it is the Torah, rather than a psychologist or counselor, mandating the separation. When the reason a couple abstain from physical relations is that God commands so, their attraction for each other grows. In contrast, when a separation is imposed for other reasons, feelings of rejection and estrangement may arise.

Indeed, the Torah's approach emphasizes that the separation is only temporary and a part of the larger goal and purpose of marriage, which is to develop a unity of spirit, an empathy, between husband and wife. The separation brought on by the *niddah* state is a necessary and useful tool, but the benefits of such a practice must be understood as enhancing the totality of the marriage experience and not be viewed as ends in themselves.

Brenda, a woman in her late thirties, appreciates the logic behind the theory of the *harchakot*. She explains:

"My husband and I have been married for twelve years and both feel we have a good, viable marriage, but there's always room for improvement. Almost by accident, we found out about the system of *Taharat Ha-Mishpachah*. We are open-minded individuals and, though we do not follow a strictly committed lifestyle, we were curious enough to try.

"Besides, society doesn't seem to offer any other reasonable, workable options to combat the possibility of a marriage going sour. Seems strange, though, because the popular 'sex-freedom' approach should have succeeded where old-fashioned modesty failed.

"We decided to give Judaism's traditional rules a try. We studied the subject and began following the laws. I must admit we did not really expect any serious changes. After all, we were basically satisfied with our relationship. Yet, enrichment came. Every visit to the *mikvah* gave us a sense of renewal and a chance to recapture the wedding night magic.

"And," adds Brenda with a wink, "for the first time in years, my husband makes a habit of calling me from work. It seems to happen precisely during the time when he can't touch me! I sense that his desire to reach out to me is a by-product of the system of the *harchakot*."

Brenda and her husband discovered how keeping the *harchakot* can help build communication between a couple by necessitating interaction of sorts other than only the physical. A husband and wife are forced to demonstrate their feelings for each other through the acts of care and regard that *are* permitted.

One of the *sheva brachot*, the wedding blessings, wishes a new couple "gladness, jubilation, joy, and delight; love, friendship, harmony, and fellowship." The great mystic Sage, the Maharal of Prague, explained the two clauses of the blessing as follows: the first clause, "gladness, jubilation, joy, and delight," applies when a woman is *tehorah*; the second, "love, friendship, harmony, and fellowship," when she is a *niddah*. We see, then, that keeping the rules of *Taharat HaMishpachah* can endow a marriage with all possible forms of happiness.

The success of a marriage revolves around these two poles of *taharah* and *niddah*. The separation of the *niddah* period teaches a couple to develop a love of friendship and harmony which finds physical expression in the dynamic and active happiness a couple experience when the woman is *tehorah*.

Indeed, the Torah desires that a man and a woman be able to express their love in a physical manner. Contrary to Christian belief, Judaism never stressed asceticism or abstinence. Nevertheless, our marriages can benefit greatly when, for a limited time, we are able to communicate only through nonphysical means. In this short span of time, different qualities, dimensions, and aspects of a relationship which otherwise may never be expressed have an opportunity to flower.

Joan and David are a couple who are, unfortunately, going through a difficult time in their marriage. They complain of disinterest and friction in their relationship.

Joan confided in her longtime friend Esther and sought her advice. Esther invited them over to spend the weekend, hoping the calm Shabbat atmosphere would be conducive to productive communication. Perhaps she and her husband would be able to help them solve a few of their difficulties.

On Friday afternoon, David and Joan arrived with their four-year-old daughter, Melanie. Throughout Shabbat, Esther noticed that the couple showered affection on one another in a very obvious manner.

When Esther and Joan began talking about Joan's marriage, Esther mentioned her observation to her friend. With an uneasy, apologetic look on her face, Joan explained, "Esther, I want you to understand that, though David and I are having problems, we haven't entirely given up on our marriage. Until we feel that it is totally unsalvageable, we really want Melanie to think that Mommy and Daddy love each other."

"What a shame," Esther thought to herself. "I wonder if all that embracing and physical closeness is the only demonstration poor Melanie sees of Daddy and Mommy's affection for each other."

There are many ways other than the physical to communicate love and regard for one's spouse. How easy it is to forget that listening attentively and respectfully to one another or simply relaxing together and sharing each other's company work to strengthen the bond between man and wife. Following the rules of the *harchakot* allows us to devote more time to these subtler forms of interpersonal communication.

The bond which the *harchakot* help to nurture in a couple's younger years will help preserve the relationship as the couple grow older. In every couple's experience, there comes a time when physical attraction and desire is no longer as powerful a motivator as it once was. What then will keep them together?

If the couple have really been communicating throughout the years of their marriage, this will not be a problem. Even in the years when the *harchakot* are no longer practiced, their beneficial influence will remain.

Once this is understood, we can return to our original premise, albeit with greater insight: the *harchakot* are the means for developing a closer, more communicative rela tionship and not a goal in their own right. Consequently, they are not practiced when a woman is *tehorah*.

A woman ought not to fear that the quality of her marriage will suffer if she is *tehorah* for a long period of time and thus does not practice the *harchakot*. This most frequently occurs when she is pregnant and, after the birth, nurses. The *harchakot* are not in and of themselves the ideal, but one of the means to achieving the ideal. The Torah wants a man and woman to express their love through physical contact during the time a woman is *tehorah*. *Hashgachah pratit,* the careful and particular manner by which God guides our lives, will determine how much of each approach—the one dictated when a woman is a *niddah* the other when she is *tehorah*—is required for each couple. Our task is to derive the maximum benefit from the possibilities offered by both types of relationship.

The *harchakot* relate very closely to the physical nature of both a husband and a wife. Men and women are different, and the Torah's rules provide an opportunity for both to become more aware of the other's natural makeup.

Vicki and Sol are a young couple who recently became committed to following the laws of *Taharat HaMishpachah*. The system as a whole appealed to them, and they considered it a worthwhile "investment" in their marriage, family, and Jewish identity. One point only Vicki could not accept—the *harchakot*.

"Look, we're doing the main things," she explained. "We abstain from marital relations while I'm a *niddah*. I carefully follow the guidelines for immersion. That's fine for me, and I think it's enough!"

Little did Vicki know how far from "fine" this was for her husband. Unwilling to rock the boat as they were both quite new at this, he held his peace. But it all came out in the open quite unexpectedly one evening.

They were having dinner with the Rabbi and his wife. Having been the ones to introduce them to the subject of *Taharat HaMishpachah*, they inquired as to how they were managing with all the detailed laws.

Vicki hesitated for a moment. "Well, we know the law really calls for total abstinence from physical contact," she said. "But we don't really keep these details. We live normally, except that we refrain from marital relations."

Vicki's husband shifted uneasily in his chair. "Actually, Rabbi, I honestly think that total observance of the laws would be better, but..."

Vicki stared at her husband uncomfortably—had she been that insensitive?—and attempted to change the subject as tactfully as possible. On the way home, Vicki and her husband finally spoke about the issue. It was only then that she realized how much a strain it was for him to "maintain and yet abstain."

The *harchakot* teach a woman to forego some of her own desires for closeness and support so as not to place her husband under unnecessary pressure and lead them both to violate the prohibition against marital relations at this time. They also give a woman a welcome opportunity for privacy.

During some of the time she is a *niddah*, a woman may naturally shy away from physical contact with her husband. Various factors, among them physical discomfort, hormonal change, and general moodiness, may cause her to seek to be alone. One sexual dysfunction researcher, writes, "At this time, women are psychologically and emotionally depressed as a result of their hormonal changes. It is not desirable for them to engage in relations with their husbands." If not for the Torah laws which obligate both of them, a woman's husband might feel slighted and regard his wife's desire for privacy as a personal insult.

A man who observes the *harchakot* does not view his wife's behavior as a disinterest in himself. Obviously, such an approach avoids much frustration and insecurity. A man's ego may be extremely sensitive, especially when the issue is his wife! The *harchakot* guarantee a woman's rights to privacy while preserving a spirit of peace and harmony within the home.

For precisely this reason, many non-Jewish observers have paid tribute to the Jewish practice of "family purity." Dr. Marie C. Stopes, an English physician who has done extensive research in the area of marital relations, explains:

> I have heard about the Jewish marital laws of *Taharat HaMishpachah*. They depict the most advanced lifestyle in the world today, being in total harmony with the functioning of a woman's body. The requirement for abstinence after menstruation and the time for resuming relations correspond precisely to the natural tides of a woman's sexual desire. Couples who adhere to these laws are sure to enjoy a happy marriage.

As in any systematic program of development, the practical application of the *harchakot* requires effort. Only through hard work can we reap the marital benefits they bring. Yet, the effort demanded by the *harchakot* differs from that of many other tasks with which we may be confronted. Most of the tests we face require us to apply ourselves to overcoming challenges from the outside. In this case, the challenge is from within: the *harchakot* teach us self-control.

Indeed, *Pirkei Avot* (4:1) teaches, "He who masters his spirit is better than one who conquers a city." Mastering desires is no simple task, for one must strike a balance between allowing one's desires to control him, and subjugating them so that the good that could come of them can show itself. Only God can define this border, and he has given us the *mitzvot*, in particular the mitzvah of *Taharat HaMishpachah*, as guides. Following the *harchakot* will enable us to control our desires without having our desires control us.

It must be remembered that the different advantages described so far cannot be considered as "the reasons for observing the *harchakot*." There is only one reason for keeping *halachot*: to fulfill God's will. As a by-product of the fulfillment of God's will, we can derive the above and other benefits.

The appreciation of the *harchakot* as first and foremost an institution of Torah law leads us to their most important function: The *harchakot* serve as a constant reminder of the wife's *niddah* state and the separation that it requires. Adherence to these rules prevents a person from transgressing the prohibition against physical contact and intimacy during the *niddah* period.

It is important to realize that these rules and standards were created by God. There are times when we might think that we could conceive of a better system, that certain rules are too strict and others allow too much closeness. But that is precisely when our faith in God and in Torah becomes important.

Debbie is a young woman who came across a pamphlet on *Taharat HaMishpachah*. It piqued her curiosity and she attended the series of lectures offered in the pamphlet. When the topic of *harchakot* was introduced, Debbie was impressed. Nevertheless, she had one basic question.

"Excuse me," she said as she raised her hand. "I'm not quite sure these rules can be accepted so universally. After all, we are dealing with a very personal subject. Take, for example, one of the laws you just described. You said that a couple mustn't simultaneously sip a drink from the same bottle when the woman is a *niddah*. But, surely, human relations vary. For one couple, that may be an act of affection. However, another might feel very uncomfortable doing that very same thing.

"Who is to say what arouses a couple's desire for intimacy? I'm sure there are couples who are not aroused by desire even when they hug and embrace."

"True," nodded the lecturer. "People's feelings vary. Indeed, what will constitute an expression of affection today might evoke a totally indifferent reaction tomorrow. There's no way that human logic could produce these rules. Knowing that is a key to understanding and appreciating these laws. Man didn't make them. God did. I don't think it's so hard to accept that the Creator knows His creation. Indeed, He knows us better than we know ourselves.

"Because these laws are part of a uniform, objective standard, there's no room to pick and choose. At times, a particular situation described by the *harchakot* may not appear as an expression of intimacy, but we must understand that the Torah's laws address themselves to the people as a whole, and individual circumstances have to be considered within this larger context.

"Besides," the lecturer concluded with a smile. "One might seriously question the relationship you described —where a hug is not an arousing gesture. The Torah encourages an intensity of feeling between husband and wife to the point where every slight touch or gesture *should* count."

Despite all the advantages the *harchakot* can bring us, there is a natural tendency to think they are restrictive. Indeed, there are many who view them as cumbersome burdens. A woman who has such feelings must be willing to accept and carry out God's will despite her own discomfort. However, she must also realize that the matter does not end there. Our Sages teach us, "The reward comes in proportion to the challenge" (*Avot* 5:23). In fact, a woman is promised ample reward for the observance of the *harchakot*: marital peace, refined children, and spiritual fulfillment. But the greatest reward may come when the woman comes to understand and appreciate this "burden" to the point where she no longer views it as such.

If you are careful during the seven days of niddah...*you will merit children who are good, friendly, and unique within their generation.*

(Or Zarua)

The Midrash describes an interesting incident which took place at the time of Creation. A delicate little animal, the dove, was brought into being and set free to roam about the newly-created universe.

The following day, the little dove confronted its Creator with a complaint: "God, why did You create me so fragile and small? My coloring is white, easily spotted by all animals of prey. My feet are so small, I can hardly escape my pursuers."

God accepted the complaint and gently attached a pair of wings to the dove's vulnerable body.

On the following day, the dove returned with a further grievance. "God, now it's even worse than before. Yesterday, it wasn't easy to run away from the predators, but, still, all I had was my own body to carry. Now, I also have to pull along these two burdensome limbs you gave me."

God smiled upon the little dove. He took her aside and patiently taught her how to use those wings. The dove learned quickly and was soon flying, soaring to the clouds.

The *harchakot* and, for that matter, the totality of Torah and *mitzvot* may occasionally appear as burdens. However, that is only because of the limited nature of our perception and our lack of knowledge of how to grow from the *mitzvot*. If we apply ourselves and become aware of God's intentions in giving us these laws, we can learn to appreciate them and use them as tools to elevate ourselves and, consequently, our marriages.

CHAPTER 7

Keeping a Distance

"DO NOT COME close to a woman who is ritually impure because of menstruation" (*VaYikra* 18:19). With this verse, the Torah prohibits not only marital relations, but all forms of physical contact—any "coming close"—from the time a woman enters the *niddah* state until after her immersion in a *mikvah*. During this time, she and her husband must observe the set of rules referred to as the *harchakot*.

Our Sages describe these rules as a "hedge of roses" (*Sanhedrin* 37a) reminding the couple of the woman's status. They have been established for our own protection. They assist a couple in preventing intimate situations which could lead to forbidden physical contact. Marital relations and other physical contact between man and wife while the woman is a *niddah* is a most serious transgression of Torah law.

The laws of *harchakot* will guide and instruct a couple how to behave in the wide variety of situations they will encounter while the woman is a *niddah*. Unless specified otherwise, these rules apply equally to both husband and wife.

Touching

1. A husband and wife may not touch each other even indirectly, that is, using an intermediate object. (For example, brushing the other's hair is forbidden.)

2. They may not touch each other's clothes while they are being worn. (Thus, one cannot brush dust off the other.)

3. A couple may not hand objects, even long ones, to each other or handle an object at the same time. (In times of great necessity, there are leniencies regarding handling very large, heavy objects and handing over a child if the child is old enough to show he wants to move to the other partner.)

4. They may not throw objects to each other, either upward in the other's direction or onto the other's lap.

5. They may not sit together on a seat which moves when sat on (e.g., a rocking chair or swing) or a sofa with one cushion, unless another person or an obvious object is placed between them.

6. When traveling for pleasure (e.g., on vacation) in a car, they may not sit on an undivided seat unless they are separated by an obvious object.

7. When traveling for business or another necessary trip, they may sit on the same seat but must avoid touching. It is advisable to place an object between them. Similarly, if the seat does not move, as in a bus, they may share a double seat but they may not touch.

Eating

1. When eating at the same table, a husband and wife must make an obvious deviation from their norm. Among the options available are

   a) Setting a food item or utensil which is not needed for that meal between their plates;
   b) the wife sitting in a different place than usual;
   c) using table mats for one or both instead of a table-cloth if the latter is the usual practice;
   d) having an additional person(s) sit with them at the table, preferably between them.

2. A couple may not eat or drink from the same plate, dish, or cup (e.g., a soda can with two straws). Therefore, when food is served on a general serving dish, they should both take food onto their individual plates and not eat directly from the serving dish. However, they may help themselves directly from bread baskets and cake or fruit platters and the like, as these are large and not taken frequently.

In contrast, foods commonly eaten "from hand to mouth" (e.g., nuts, dried fruit, or the like) must be placed on individual settings, or another person must help himself to some of the food in between the couple helping themselves.

3. A husband may not eat or drink from his wife's leftovers in her presence, even if more food is added to the plate. If someone else has eaten from her leftovers first, they have been transferred to another plate, or she has left the room, he may eat them.

4. If he does not know that the leftovers on a certain dish are hers, she is not obligated to tell him, and he may eat them. If she ate only one kind of food from among the foods on her plate, the remainder are not considered her leftovers.

5. A wife may eat or drink from her husband's leftovers.

6. A husband or wife may not serve food or pour drinks for each other unless they do so in a fashion which shows a deviation from their usual manner (e.g., serving with the left hand or setting down the plate slightly removed from the spouse's place).

7. They should not pour wine for one another at all. (There is no problem with a wife drinking from her husband's kiddush cup as long as he places it on the table and does not direct it specifically to her.)

Bedroom Arrangements

1. The couple must sleep in separate beds. A double bed that does not separate into two cannot be used no matter how large it is.

2. Space must be made between the two beds so that neither the beds nor the bedding touch. During the day, the beds may touch when they are not being used.

3.   A husband may not sit or lie on his wife's bed, even if she is not present in the room, as long as she is in town.

4.   A wife may not lie on her husband's bed in his presence, but she may sit on it. When he is not present, she may lie on it.

5.   They may not prepare each other's bed for sleeping in each other's presence.

Washing and Bathing

1.   A couple may not prepare water for each other to wash or bathe with (or even add water to the bathtub) in the other's presence. (They may prepare water for *negel vasser*, the required morning washing.)

Additional Restrictions

1.   A husband and wife may not engage in flirtatious behavior that may lead to sexual desire. (Obviously, this does not mean that during the time the woman is a *niddah*, she and her husband must appear grumpy or sour faced!)
     During this time, a woman should take care to appear attractive, but not provocative, to her husband.

2.   A husband may not see parts of his wife's body that are usually covered. Thus, a woman must not undress in front of her husband.

3.   He may not smell her perfume, whether it is on her or on her clothes.

4. He may not listen to her singing.

5. They should not discuss intimate subjects or talk about things which may arouse sexual desire. Study and clarification of the *niddah* laws at this time is permitted.

6. A couple must observe the *harchakot* even when one of them is sick and the other is taking care of him or her. Nevertheless, a case of *piku'ach nefesh,* threat to life or limb, takes precedence over these laws.

CHAPTER 8

The Mysterious Waters

MRS. KLEIN AND her daughter Rosa were the only members of their family who, after much hardship, finally emigrated from behind the Iron Curtain. Mrs. Klein's husband Samuel had passed away in Russia, and their son Joseph, a physicist, was not granted a visa.

Weary but hopeful, the two women began a new life in Israel. Rosa attended high school and continued her studies in a teachers' seminary. Upon graduating, she delighted her mother by announcing her engagement to a fine young man.

After one particularly tiring day of errands and shopping, Mrs. Klein and her daughter spent the evening relaxing in their living room. Mrs. Klein was in an expansive mood and began to reminisce about life in Russia.

"You know, Rosa," she said, "there is no way you can appreciate how happy your father would be to know that his daughter is getting married in Eretz Yisrael and preparing to live a life of Torah and *mitzvot*.

"You were a young girl when we still lived ٦ Russia, and there were many secrets we were forced to keep from you. One of them was that, in our basement, we maintained a *mikvah* which enabled forty Jewish families in our village to keep the laws of *Taharat HaMishpachah*.

"You cannot imagine the enormous effort and constant danger such a project involved. From the moment we started building, we had to hide our doings from the KGB. Your father built most of the *mikvah* himself. Nevertheless, how does one hide hundreds of kilograms of cement from nosy neighbors?˙ And, of course, the *mikvah* had to be 100% kosher. Your father would have it no other way. He contacted a Rabbi from faraway Moscow and offered to pay his entire fare if he would come and guide him in the construction. At first, the Rabbi was reluctant. The penalty for such a crime, should they be detected, was certain death. But your father begged him and the Rabbi agreed."

"And the neighbors never found out?" asked Rosa in amazement.

"Well, we did have some close calls," replied her mother. "Once, a troublesome neighbor was determined to find out where the trapdoor at the bottom of the staircase led. He came upon your father just as he was changing the water.

"'Hello, Mr. Klein! What is this?'

"Your father looked up, the calm expression on his face disclosing none of his inner fears. 'Oh, it's you,

Gregory! As you know, we often have trouble with our water supply in this building. I got fed up and decided to construct my own private well. I didn't want anyone to find out, otherwise we'd be bombarded every time there is a shortage!'

"Gregory continued to eye him with obvious suspicion. Your father then scooped up a cupful of the water which forty families had used in the *mikvah* for almost a year. 'It's very tasty,' he continued, downing the whole cup. 'Can I offer you a drink?' Declining the offer, Gregory retreated, no longer curious. Your father followed after him: 'If you promise not to tell anyone, I'll let you use this well when there's a shortage.'"

Rosa smiled at her father's ingenuity, but her face quickly turned serious: "Mother, how could you have lived with such constant fear?"

Mrs. Klein replied quietly: "How could we have lived otherwise?"

The concepts of *taharah*, ritual purity, and *tumah*, impurity, given us in the Torah transcend our comprehension. As the Rambam explains: "It is clear that the laws of ritual purity and impurity are decrees of the Torah that cannot be comprehended by human wisdom..." (*Hilchot Mikvaot* 11:12). Because these concepts are divine in nature, the transition from the state of *tumah* (of being a *niddah*) to the state of *taharah* must by definition be a Godly process. The culmination of this process involves preparation for and immersion in the *mikvah*. Acting on faith alone, Jewish families throughout the ages have been willing to put their lives on the line in order that women may immerse and lead lives of purity and devotion to God.

What Is a *Mikvah*?

The word *mikvah* literally means "collection." In the Torah's discussion of the laws of ritual purity and impurity, it states, "Nevertheless, a spring or a cistern where there is a collection [*mikvah*] of water shall be pure" (*Vayikra* 11:36).

Based on this verse and other teachings, our Sages have articulated the detailed laws governing the construction of a pool containing this "collection of water." Throughout the centuries, wherever Jews have lived, they have followed these laws and constructed *mikvaot*. So vital is this structure to the life of a Jewish community that Torah law requires its construction to precede the building of a synagogue or purchasing a Torah scroll.

Today, a *mikvah* building will contain this pool of water (many *mikvaot* have a number of pools), bathing rooms and showers, and a waiting room. Many *mikvaot* are also equipped with saunas and offer extras ranging from hairdressing accessories to individual makeup rooms. Being women, we can appreciate these extras which beautify the mitzvah and contribute to a pleasurable experience.

However, we must not let these "extras" cause us to lose sight of the fundamentally spiritual nature of the *mikvah* experience. Going to the *mikvah* is essentially a process of spiritual transition to a state of ritual purity. How far this idea is from the widespread misconception which links the term *tumah* to uncleanliness. It is spiritual impurity and not actual dirt which we wash away with our immersions.

It is difficult to understand how such a misconception could have arisen. It is mandatory to bathe very thoroughly *before* immersing in the *mikvah*, as explained in the laws detailed in the next chapter. Immersion in the *mikvah* has been required by the Torah on many other occasions when personal cleanliness was not the issue. For example, before the giving of the Torah on Mount Sinai, the entire Jewish people were instructed to immerse in a *mikvah*. When the priests were initiated into service in the Temple, and, frequently as part of that service, they were required to immerse in a *mikvah*. The High Priest was commanded to immerse himself in a *mikvah* five times on Yom Kippur. The process of conversion to Judaism requires immersion in a *mikvah*.

From these examples we can gather a clearer idea of the mitzvah's function: to facilitate the transition to a new spiritual status and to sensitize our bodies to a higher level of holiness.

In all *mitzvot*, the form which the mitzvah is to take—how it is performed—and the result desired from its performance are inseparable. The only way we can attain the spiritual heights to which the Torah leads us is by using the specific tools which God has designed. Would anyone suggest blowing a trumpet instead of a shofar?

Similarly, a *mikvah* is not a glorified bathtub, sauna, or swimming pool. Yes, cleanliness is important to the mitzvah of immersion, but only as a preparatory step. In no way can the bath, this act of preparation, take the place of the *mikvah*, the process of spiritual transformation for which the bath merely readies us. The divinely-ordained change of status from *tumah* to *taharah* must be carried out using the divinely-prescribed tool, the *mikvah*. The Rambam summarizes this issue: "Immersion is also a matter which must be accepted on faith...for ritual impurity is not mud or filth which washes off with water" (*Hilchot Mikvaot* 11:12).

Ruth is a *Taharat HaMishpachah* counselor who teaches women the subject on an individual basis. Rabbis often recommend her name to brides who need to learn the laws in preparation for their marriage. Often, Ruth accompanies "her" brides to the *mikvah* in order to provide assistance and encouragement if necessary.

Once, the mother of one of the brides Ruth had taught accompanied the two to the *mikvah*. While the bride bathed before immersion, Ruth joined the mother in the waiting room.

"You know," the mother said as they were waiting, "my daughter has been sharing some of your ideas with me. I'm really quite impressed."

"They're not my ideas," smiled Ruth. "They're the Torah's. I'm just trained to explain them to others. As a matter of fact, not long ago, the passing on of this heritage was strictly a mother-daughter affair."

"Yes, I know," nodded the mother. "My mother taught me the rules and laws of *Taharat HaMishpachah* and I still follow some of them."

Ruth looked at the woman in surprise. She knew the bride's family was "traditional," but that was a far cry from observing the *mitzvot*.

The mother continued: "I separate from my husband for the required amount of time. I count the days and even do the personal inspections. It's only the *mikvah* I leave out. I just take a bath at the end of the seven days. You see, I feel the requirement to immerse in a *mikvah* was appropriate for my mother's time, but we live in a much more modern world, and sanitary conditions are of a higher standard."

Ruth had heard this argument before. She was about to answer and explain when, suddenly, the woman continued:

"Isn't it strange—tonight is the right time for me to take my bath." Ruth immediately perked up. "What a remarkable coincidence," she thought. "Forget the rational discussions and arguments! This woman is going to immerse in the *mikvah* tonight!" she decided.

It did not take too much convincing. The mother herself was inspired by the extraordinary turn of events. A short while later, she entered the bathing room, received basic instruction, and, for the first time in her life, the woman immersed in a *mikvah*. As she drove home that night, Ruth mused to herself: "What a strange generation we are living in. Like daughter, like mother..."

The lesson Ruth taught the bride's mother is clearly expressed by the Rambam:

> If [a woman] washed in a bath, even if all the waters in the world passed over her, she remains in precisely the same condition as before bathing...as nothing except the immersion in a mikvah changes the status from impure to pure.
>
> (Hilchot Issurei Biah *11:16*).

Her whole married life, this woman had preferred to think that these laws were no longer relevant because she did not understand the reason for them. Yes, we must accept the basic principles of ritual purity and impurity and immersion on faith. Nevertheless, a thorough examination of these laws will reveal a number of profound philosophical insights which add to our understanding of the issue. Indeed, Jewish phi-

losophy and mysticism have devoted much thought to discovering these insights.

Many laws pertaining to *tumah* revolve around the ab-
sence of life. For example, contact with a human corpse or
the carcass of an animal renders a person *tamei*.

When a woman begins to menstruate, she, too, experiences a loss of life. A month has gone by in which she has
not conceived, and the egg readied for that purpose has
gone unused. The Torah considers this loss of potential life a
source of *tumah*.

In contrast, water is the source of all life. God created the
world from water. All living entities require water for their
survival. An embryo develops enclosed in a sac of water.

The divine commandment of immersion in a *mikvah* can
be seen as a transition from a connection to death to the
renewal of life. Beneath the *mikvah's* waters, a woman
rejuvenates herself and once again becomes a potential
partner with God and her husband in the act of creation. She
emerges from the life-giving waters "born anew" and ready to
conceive anew.

*Each and every month, a woman renews herself by immersing
in the* mikvah *and returns to her husband as dear to him as on
the day of the wedding. Just as the moon renews itself each
Rosh Chodesh, and all wait to see her, so a woman becomes
renewed each month, and her husband awaits her and she is
dear to him like a new wife.*

(Pirkei DeRabbi Elazar)

"I remember," recalls Toby, "the first time I had to go to
the *mikvah*. I was so reluctant; the whole idea seemed
strange and foreign to me. But I had no choice about the

matter. My fiance insisted that I go at least the one time before our wedding.

"I was determined to make it a quick dip and get out of there as soon as possible! Strangely enough, I found myself enjoying every moment. As I descended the steps and slowly immersed in the water, a sense of rejuvenation overtook me.

"I was overwhelmed by the experience and needed to express my new feelings. As if reading my thoughts, the attendant presented me with a lovely prayer inscribed in a pamphlet.

"There I was, sitting on the couch in the waiting room reading the booklet, when I heard a familiar honk from outside. I thanked the attendant and hurried outside. My mother was waiting in the car.

"'What took you so long?' she asked, 'You said it would take only a minute.'

"'I don't know, Ma. I swore this would be my first and last time. I planned on jumping in and out just to please Jack, but somehow I got "immersed" in the mikvah experience. I have a feeling this won't be my last time either.'"

As stated earlier, it is not just any water that is capable of bringing about the transition from tumah to taharah. A bath, shower, or another type of pool cannot serve as a mikvah. What is so unique about the mikvah's waters?

Most of us think "water is water." However, any tourist knows that the water in the country he is visiting tastes very different from the water at home. Scientists have discovered a tangible physical difference between ordinary water and heavy water. Is it so farfetched to comprehend differences between the spiritual nature of one body of water and that of another? He who commanded the *mikvah* waters to purify did not command so concerning tap water.

The laws concerning the erection of a kosher *mikvah* provide an insight into the spiritual nature of the *mikvah's* waters. The pool in which we immerse ourselves is filled with fresh tap water. Connected to that pool is a cistern containing rain or well water; this water cannot have been contained within a movable vessel or carried by human hands. Thus, the water in which we immerse is connected to water that comes directly from a natural source.

The connection to these natural waters alludes to a connection with the primeval waters of creation. The spiritual message of such an association is obvious. As our great Sage Shammai said: "Great is the woman who observes the laws of *niddah*. They separate her from sin and bring her close to *Gan Eden*" (*Niddah* 81a).

Rabbi Shuster is the leader of a Jewish community in Southern California. After many months of determined effort, a beautiful *mikvah* building was dedicated in the posh suburban neighborhood. Many a synagogue member was skeptical as to the extent of its planned use and popularity.

Rabbi Shuster looked at the matter from a different perspective. He had given many lectures, classes, and workshops discussing the topic of *Taharat HaMishpachah*. He felt that an attractive modern *mikvah* would boost the practical application of the theoretical principles he had been teaching.

Despite the many obstacles he had to overcome, all went well for the good Rabbi except for...the weather!

The expected rain had not fallen, and the *mikvah* could not be filled. In Southern California, heavy rains fall only a few months a year, so it seemed as if there was no choice but to wait for the next rainy season.

But Rabbi Shuster was not to be discouraged. He would not take "wait" for an answer when it came to the observance of *mitzvot!* "Is there no other alternative?" he asked a prominent halachic authority.

After investigating the matter in depth, they arrived at a possible solution. There is a mishnah in Tractate *Mikvaot* (7:1) which teaches that a *mikvah* can be made from snow. As long as it does not melt before it is placed in the *mikvah*, it is considered "natural water" and may be used. There was plenty of snow atop the peaks of the Sierras! Cases of fresh snow could be packed and shipped down south in refrigerated trucks.

What a sight to behold! Two bearded gentlemen, black hats on their heads and with the distinguished look of the Rabbinate about them, were standing atop a mountain peak in large rubber boots, packing snow into wire carriers. The truck drivers had quite a story to tell when they returned.

And little did the women who used the *mikvah* back home know that what enabled them to enjoy a warm, comfortable immersion was a snowy mountain top a hundred miles away.

Atop the towering desert fortress of Masada, archaeologists have discovered two thousand-year-old *mikvaot* with a structure similar to that of present-day *mikvaot*. Despite the lack of rain, provisions were made to construct kosher *mikvaot*. Rabbi Shuster's problem was not unique; rather, we see from both cases the lengths gone to in order to insure the connection with all-natural waters, which is the very essence of the *mikvah*.

A fundamental tenet of Judaism is the sanctification of time. Men achieve this sanctification through performance of the time-bound *mitzvot*. Women, however, are freed of the requirement to perform the positive time-bound *mitzvot*. Due to the regular occurrence and reoccurrence of their menstrual cycle, women are by nature more conscious of the passage of time. If a woman sanctifies this monthly cycle by immersion in the *mikvah,* she also simultaneously achieves a sanctification of time and thereby accomplishes that which men are required to do through the performance of the time-bound *mitzvot*.

Our Sages have greatly stressed the requirement to immerse in the *mikvah* "on time," at the end of the seven spotless days. They have elaborated on the immense merit and reward deserved by a woman who sanctifies time by immersing on time. Rav Yitzchak Luria, the Saintly Ari, declared, "From time to time, souls with great spiritual potentials are drawn down to this world. Who merits to conceive them? Women who immerse on time."

Karen had been married for nine long years, during which she was unable to experience the joys of motherhood. Although she had undergone various treatments, she was unable to conceive. During this time, she and her husband discovered the system of *Taharat HaMishpachah*. They contacted a *Taharat HaMishpachah* counselor and Karen studied with her. The couple soon realized that their adherence to these laws could enrich their marriage and determined to follow them. "At least we'll have paid our dues to God," thought Karen. "Maybe He will 'repay' us for our effort."

Months passed by. Karen and her husband were very pleased with the "investment" they had made: their marriage was better than ever. "Hope for a child—well, that would be a pure gift," thought Karen.

One late winter night, the telephone rang in the home of the *Taharat HaMishpachah* counselor. It was Karen.

"Oh, Mrs. Lane!" she cried in exasperation. "Everything seems to have gone wrong for me today. Tonight is my time to immerse in the *mikvah*, but I just can't make it. My refrigerator broke down, and I spent hours trying to get a repair man. I finally drove out to the company myself but got stuck in a traffic jam. Then my in-laws arrived for a supper that wasn't cooked....

"My head is spinning. I remember you teaching me that a woman should not postpone her immersion, but couldn't this time be an exception? I'm not in the mood. Besides, by now the *mikvah* is probably locked, and it's snowing outside. I just can't handle anything else tonight!"

The counselor calmed her and reminded her of the importance of immersing on time. Her gentle tone and relaxed response helped Karen regain her equilibrium. Yet, it didn't seem possible. "But it's too late now, and I haven't even prepared myself," argued Karen.

Mrs. Lane assured her that it would be okay. "I'll call the *mikvah* attendant and make a special request. We won't even trouble her to come down. I have a key. I'll take you myself and supervise you as required."

"But it's 10:30 at night and snowing outside."

The counselor was not to be dissuaded. "Give me a ring when you're ready. I'll be waiting by my door."

Karen could not believe this woman's devotion. How could she refuse her generous offer? Few other cars ventured out that snowy night, but Karen, driving slowly in her blue sedan, was one of them.

Later that night, Karen could not help feeling pleased with herself. She had gone to the *mikvah* on time despite the odds against her. She had even more reason to be pleased when she gave birth to a lovely daughter exactly nine months later.

Immersion in the *mikvah* differs from all other *mitzvot* in one crucial way. All other *mitzvot* involve the usage of just one limb or some other part of the body: *Tefillin* are placed on the arm and head; *matzah* is eaten. By contrast, as a women descends the steps of the *mikvah* and lowers her body into the water she is entirely "immersed" in the fulfillment of a mitzvah.

This principle is reflected in the laws requiring us to avoid any kind of *chatzitzah*, intervening substance, that might prevent complete contact with the water. Nothing must stand between the woman and the water that enables her to change her status from *tumah* to *taharah*.

As the Rambam states: "A woman cannot emerge from the state of impurity...until she immerses in the waters of a kosher *mikvah* without having anything intervening between her flesh and the water" (*Hilchot Issurei Biah* 11:16). But a deeper point is indicated here. Immersion in the *mikvah* represents a bond with the source of all existence, God. A woman who immerses so that her entire body is covered by the waters of the *mikvah* is relating totally, with her entire being, to God. It is only after such a totality of commitment that one can become purified.

It was a rainy, grey Friday afternoon, as a small group of people trudged up the winding, muddy road to the Mount of Olives. The wife of Dr. Kahn, a longtime resident of Jerusalem, had passed away, and a few of the family's friends and relatives were making their way to the funeral.

Huddled around the freshly dug grave, the ten men required for the ceremony were anxious for it to begin. The heavy rains and approaching Shabbat called for no delay. Nevertheless, the attendants were reluctant to lower the coffin into the grave. At least two feet of water had collected inside it.

Nothing could be done but wait for the rain to subside. Nearly an hour had passed, and still there was no sign of the shower diminishing. Try as they would, the attendants could not empty the grave. As soon as they bailed the water out, the rains refilled it.

Discouraged, drenched, and increasingly worried as sunset neared, they decided to proceed as best they could. The coffin was lowered manually and held tight as the grave was filled.

One could not help but notice the tears streaming down Dr. Kahn's face. A friend put his arm around his shoulder and supported his trembling frame, groping for words of comfort. Dr. Kahn shook his head.

"I'm not questioning the ways of God," he said. "I'm just thinking of these unusual circumstances. We led a traditional Jewish lifestyle, but my wife refused to follow the laws of *Taharat HaMishpachah*. She never went to the *mikvah*. Is it not an ironic coincidence that upon death, she 'merited' a total immersion in a naturally made *mikvah*?"

A woman must see immersion in the *mikvah* as more than a rite to be carefully performed. In the physical act of immersion, the *mikvah's* waters must cover the woman totally. Similarly, from an emotional perspective, the woman must be totally submerged in the experience of *mikvah*. She must appreciate it as a holy process, granting her new sensitivity to spirituality. The sense of *taharah*, the anticipated reunion with her husband and, most importantly, the satisfaction of fulfilling God's will, all combine to create an uplifting experience. With the proper attitude, a woman will find that she can immerse herself with true *simchah shel mitzvah*, the joy of fulfilling a mitzvah.

God is described as *Mikveh Yisrael*, literally, "the Hope of Israel" (*Yirmiyahu* 17:13). Rabbi Akiva develops the connection between that term and our mitzvah, explaining: "Rejoice, O Israel....See who purifies you—your Father in heaven, as it states...'God is the *Mikvah* of Israel.' Just as a *mikvah* purifies the impure, so God purifies Israel" (*Yoma* 85).

The Torah concepts are interrelated: When Israel appreciates that it is God who purifies her, she can face the future with true hope and confidence. A woman who immerses in the *mikvah* recognizes that it is God who purifies, so she, too, can look forward to the future full of hope and confidence.

תְּפִילָה לִפְנֵי הַטְּבִילָה

רִבּוֹנוֹ שֶׁל עוֹלָם, בְּלֵב רָגִישׁ אֲנִי מְקַיֶּמֶת מִצְוַת
טְבִילָה לְשֵׁם טָהֳרָה. הִשְׁתַּדַּלְתִּי לִהְיוֹת נֶאֱמָנָה
לְמִצְוֹתֶיךָ וּמְצַפָּה לִישׁוּעָתֶךָ, וּכְשֵׁם שֶׁמֵּי הַמִּקְוֶה
מְטַהֲרִים אוֹתִי מִבְּחִינָה רוּחָנִית, כַּךְ אֲנִי מִתְפַּלֶּלֶת
אֵלֶיךָ שֶׁתִּשְׁטוֹף מֵעָלַי כָּל עֲבֵרָה וְעָוֹן וְכָל עֶצֶב
וְיָגוֹן.

רִבּוֹנוֹ שֶׁל עוֹלָם, אֲשֶׁר בְּיָדְךָ נֶפֶשׁ כָּל חַי, חוֹנֵן
אוֹתִי וְאֶת בַּעֲלִי (וּבְנֵי מִשְׁפַּחְתִּי) וְאֶת כָּל קְרוֹבַי וְאֶת
כָּל עַם יִשְׂרָאֵל מִבִּרְכוֹתֶיךָ, לְחַיִּים אֲרֻכִּים בְּרִיאוּת
אוֹשֶׁר וּמַזָּל טוֹב (וְנַחַת מִבָּנִים) וְתַשְׁרֶה עָלַי אֶת
רוּחֲךָ הַטְּהוֹרָה וּשְׁכִינַת קָדְשֶׁךָ.

וִיהִי רָצוֹן שֶׁיְּהֵא בֵּיתֵנוּ בַּיִת שֶׁל שָׁלוֹם אַהֲבָה
וְאַחְוָה וְחַסְדֶּךָ לֹא יָסוּר מֵעִמָּנוּ נֶצַח וְאֶהְיֶה תָּמִיד
רְאוּיָה לְטָהֳרָה הָרְאוּיָה לִנְשֵׁי עַמְּךָ בֵּית יִשְׂרָאֵל אָמֵן.

Suggested Prayer before Immersion

Master of the world: With an inspired heart, I approach the fulfillment of the mitzvah of immersion for the sake of purity. I have made an effort to be faithful to Your *mitzvot* and I look forward to Your salvation. Just as the *mikvah's* waters purify me spiritually, I pray to You to wash away from me all sin and transgression, all sadness and sorrow.

Master of the world, in whose hand are the souls of all living beings, grant me, my husband, (my family), all my relations, and the totality of the Jewish people Your blessings for long life, health, good fortune (and, satisfaction from their children). May Your pure spirit and Your Holy *Shechinah* rest upon me.

May it be Your will that our house be a house of peace, love, and closeness. May Your grace never depart from us, and may I always be worthy of the purity appropriate to the women of Your Nation, the House of Israel. Amen.

CHAPTER 9

Taking the Plunge

The Proper Time for *Tevilah*—Immersion in The *Mikvah*

1. AT THE END of the seven spotless days and nights, a woman is obligated to immerse in the *mikvah*. For example: If the *hefsek taharah* was performed on Monday afternoon, Tuesday would be the first of the seven spotless days. The following Monday night would be the time for immersion.

2. A woman should only immerse in the *mikvah* at night, after at least three stars are visible. This law applies even when, for some valid reason, she is forced to postpone her immersion. If it is totally impossible to immerse at night, a Rav must be consulted.

3. If a woman's husband is out of town, it is preferable that she postpone her immersion until his return. Nevertheless, the halacha allows her to immerse regardless.

4. The requirement to immerse on time also applies on Friday night if a woman's husband is in town. However, she

should not immerse Friday night if her husband is not in town.

5. A woman who was scheduled to immerse before Friday night and postponed her immersion without a valid reason may not immerse Friday night. Nevertheless, it is advisable to consult a Rav in such a case.

6. On Yom Kippur, the fast of the 9th of Av, and during her *shivah* week of mourning, a woman may not immerse, even if it is her appropriate time.

7. A husband planning to go out of town should try to postpone his departure if he had intended to leave home at the time of his wife's immersion.

The Laws of *Chafifah*—The Preparations Which Precede Immersion

The mitzvah of immersion requires a thorough preparation before actually entering the *mikvah*. This process of preparation is referred to as *chafifah*. It involves

1. thorough bathing;

2. inspecting oneself for any possible *chatzitzot*—substances that prevent total body contact with the *mikvah* waters.

The halacha requires that a woman's entire body be submerged in the *mikvah*'s water. Nothing should separate her from the waters. The body's "hidden parts" need not come into actual contact with the water. However, they, too, must be cleaned to the extent that no foreign substances are found upon them. This applies to a woman's mouth, teeth, nose, eyes, ears, nipples, navel, anus, and vagina. All dirt and foreign substances must be removed from these areas before immersion.

The Preparation Process

1.   A woman should remove all hairpins and unbraid her hair. She must wash her hair with *warm* water and shampoo (not a kind that causes tangling). Afterwards, she should carefully comb out her hair while wet, removing any snarls or knots. She should comb or separate by hand other body hair, including eyebrows, eyelashes, underarm and pubic hair.

2.   A woman should bathe in a tub, washing all parts of her body with warm water and soap (only soaps which rinse off totally should be used). It is best to soak in a warm bath for half an hour. The entire preparation process should take about an hour. In time of great urgency, half an hour is sufficient. If such a case should occur, extra care should be taken with the inspection afterward. (When bathing is ab-solutely impossible, a woman may take a shower. However, this should be done meticulously, using sufficient soap and water.)

3.   Ideally, a woman should begin the *chafifah* by day, carrying on through nightfall to the time of immersion. If a woman cannot begin by day, she may bathe at night, pre-ferably for an hour, with care and proper attention. It is better to bathe relaxedly and slowly at night than to bathe in a hurry during the day. Nevertheless, ideally, she should

carry out at least some form of preparation during the day (for example, washing her hair or cutting her nails).

4.   Bathing should be done as close to the time of immersing as possible.

5.   It is customary to wash and comb at the *mikvah*. All *mikvaot* provide proper facilities for bathing. Nevertheless, a woman may prepare herself at home and, then, comb out her hair again at the *mikvah*.

6.   Meat and chicken should not be eaten on the day of immersion because particles may stick between teeth and be difficult to remove. If the day of her immersion falls on Shabbat or a Festival (when eating meat is a mitzvah), or if a woman forgot this restriction, she must clean her teeth with extra care.

7.   A woman should not knead dough on the day of her immersion. If it was *erev* Shabbat and she customarily bakes her own challah, or if she forgot, she must take extra care to clean all particles of dough from her hands.

8.   A woman should not eat between *chafifah* and immersion.

9.   Both fingernails and toenails must be cut and cleaned. One must be careful not to forget a nail or part of it. (In certain instances, leniency may be granted to a woman who insists on keeping her nails long. However, a Rav must be consulted.) Remove nail polish, false nails, and the like.

10.   A woman should blow her nose and use the bathroom, when necessary, before immersion.

11. All jewelry (earrings, rings, etc.), contact lenses, glasses, makeup, creams, and band-aids should be removed.

12. The ears, including earring holes, should be cleaned thoroughly.

13. The teeth must be brushed, and an additional cleansing tool (a toothpick or dental floss) should be used. All removable false teeth should be taken out before immersion.

14. A woman is obligated to check (by looking at and feeling) her body and hair before immersing to verify that there is no *chatzitzah*. Neglecting to inspect invalidates her immersion.

15. Immersion on Friday night requires special care because of the laws of Shabbat. A woman may not bathe and comb her hair too late on Friday lest she violate the Shabbat. She may bathe at the *mikvah*, but she must be careful to finish a couple of minutes before sunset. Her husband can light the candles for her or she can light early on condition that she does not accept upon herself the onset of Shabbat until the correct time. In the latter instance, before sunset she should say, "I hereby accept upon myself the sanctity of Shabbat."

16. Immersion on Saturday night requires that *chafifah* have been done on Friday afternoon and, then, repeated Saturday night. If that is impossible, it may all be done on Saturday night. However, in such an instance, a woman should bathe for an hour before immersing.

17. A woman whose immersion is scheduled for a Friday night which follows a two-day Festival should consult a Rav for instructions as to how and when to do *chafifah*.

18. The process of *chafifah* should be done calmly and with ease. Do not rush! Relax!

Laws of *Chatzitzah*

Proper immersion in the *mikvah* requires that every part of the body comes into contact with the water. All *chatzitzot* must be removed. Some examples of common types of *chatzitzot* are discussed below. Obviously, this book cannot cover every possible situation that may arise. One should always consult a Rav when in doubt.

Chatzitzot of the Hair

Body hair: A woman who regularly removes certain body hair, for example, shaving underarms, tweezing eyebrows, or waxing legs must do so before going to the *mikvah* but preferably not on the very day she immerses. (Sephardic woman customarily remove underarm and pubic hair before immersion.)

Dandruff or lice: A woman must do the maximum to remove excess dandruff or lice before immersion.

Dyes: Some hair dyes are considered *chatzitzot*. The decision depends on the substance used as a dye. A Rav must be consulted.

Hair conditioner: It is preferable not to use hair conditioners prior to immersion.

Chatzitzot of the Body

Callouses and hardened skin: The determination of whether or not these are considered a *chatzitzah* depends on the woman's attitude. If she would normally remove them, they are considered a *chatzitzah*. If she would not usually bother to remove them, they are not a *chatzitzah*.

Color stains on the skin (e.g. ink, blood, breast milk, paint): When a woman would not normally mind the stain, it is only considered a *chatzitzah* if dry. In such an instance, she must wash it in warm water. If she would normally be disturbed by such a stain and attempt to remove it, it is considered a *chatzitzah* whether dry or moist. She must then scrub it off as best she can. Any residue is not considered a *chatzitzah*.

Discharge from a sore: A dry substance is considered a *chatzitzah*; a moist substance is not.

Ears and Nose: A dry substance found on the outer area is considered a *chatzitzah*; on the inner area, it is not. All substances should be removed from the openings to these parts of the body.

Eyes: Any substance found on the outside of the eye, whether dry or moist, is considered a *chatzitzah*. Inside the eye, a dry substance is considered a *chatzitzah*, a moist one is not.

Hanging skin: Hanging skin is considered a *chatzitzah* if the woman would usually seek to remove it; otherwise, it is not. Nevertheless, in all cases, it is proper to remove large pieces that can be removed easily. Peeling skin should be smoothed and any skin that bothers the woman removed. The remainder may be left as is.

Pus: Pus which is from a sore and beneath the skin is not considered a *chatzitzah*. Different rules apply if it is on the surface of skin. For the first three days, it is not considered a *chatzitzah*, if moist. Afterwards, or when dry, it is considered a *chatzitzah* and must be softened by soaking.

Scabs: A scab covering a wound that has not healed should be softened by soaking. It is not considered a *chatzitzah* and need not be removed. If the sore has healed, the scab is a *chatzitzah*.

Splinters: A splinter beneath the skin is not considered a *chatzitzah*. On the skin surface or above, it is considered a *chatzitzah*.

Teeth: Permanent caps, bridges, and fillings are not considered *chatzitzot*. A Rav should be consulted in regard to temporary fillings or caps.

In general, the definition of what constitutes a *chatzitzah* depends upon the attitude of women towards the situation in question. A substance that would bother the majority of women and make them anxious to remove it, even if only occasionally, is considered a *chatzitzah*. This law applies regardless of an individual's attitude. Conversely, the presence of a questionable substance which bothers an individual, even if it would not necessarily bother the majority of women, is considered a *chatzitzah* for that individual.

Laws of *Tevilah*

1.   Upon completing her bathing preparations and inspecting herself for any *chatzitzot,* she must immerse her entire body in a kosher *mikvah.* The *mikvah* must contain enough water to reach at least 24 cm. (9.5 inches) above her navel when she is standing erect.

2.   In order to ensure that her body and hair are totally submerged in the *mikvah,* an attendant (a Jewish female above the age of twelve) supervises the immersion. If no attendant is available, the woman should consult a Rav.

3.   The immersion must be performed while maintaining complete contact with the water and keeping the body relaxed. Therefore, a woman should not

   a)   hold on to anyone or press forcefully against the wall;
   b)   clench her fists or feet;
   c)   close her mouth very tightly;
   d)   shut her eyes very tightly.

(In case of problematic situations [e.g., a woman physically unable to support herself or afraid of submerging in water], a Rav should be consulted for a possible solution. It is worthwhile to note that recently a *mikvah* specially designed to be used by women who are physically disabled and unable to walk was constructed in Jerusalem.)

4.   A woman should not immerse totally upright or bent. Rather, she should lean forward slightly as if kneading dough. She should spread her legs and arms in a normal walking position and should not hold them close against her body.

5. After immersing once, a woman should stand in the *mikvah* and recite the following blessing:

בָּרוּךְ אַתָּה ה' אֱלֹהֵינוּ מֶלֶךְ הָעוֹלָם אֲשֶׁר קִדְּשָׁנוּ בְּמִצְוֹתָיו וְצִוָּנוּ עַל הַטְּבִילָה.

Blessed are You, God, our Lord, King of the world, who has sanctified us with His commandments and commanded us concerning immersion.

Afterwards, she should immerse again. It is common practice to immerse three times. (Some woman follow different customs which require additional immersions.)

While reciting the blessing, it is customary

a) not to look into the water;
b) to cover one's hair with a towel;
c) to loosely fold one's arms across the waist so as to separate the upper and lower parts of the body.

The custom of some Sephardic women is to recite the blessing before entering the room of the *mikvah* pool.

6. The *mikvah* attendant confirms the immersion by pronouncing "kosher," meaning halachically acceptable. The woman should then glance at the attendant.

The act of immersion should be kept as a private matter between husband and wife. No other people should know of it. Upon greeting her husband after immersing, a woman should inform him that she has immersed (verbally or by some other indication). Just as she previously announced her entry into the state of *niddah* to him, so, now, she informs him of her change of status to that of *taharah*.

At times when a regular *mikvah* is unavailable, a Rav should be consulted for instructions concerning the use of other acceptable bodies of water (e.g., spring fed lakes or the sea). These alternatives are not desirable and should only be used under exceptional circumstances. In these instances:

1. Do not stand in a narrow place or step where the possibility of falling exists.

2. Follow the Rav's instructions concerning a suitable surface on which to stand when immersing.

3. Choose a private area for the immersion.

The *Mikvah* Attendant

Although every woman is responsible to wash and inspect herself in preparation for immersion, the halacha comes to her assistance in this process by requiring that a *mikvah* attendant be available to help and supervise. The attendant confirms a woman's readiness to immerse and supervises the immersion, assuring that it is properly done (e.g., watching that not a single hair floats above the water).

Mrs Rabinowitz's daughter Leah was about to be married. She insisted that her daughter have the very best *Taharat HaMishpachah* instructor. Leah could not understand why her mother was making such a fuss over the choice of a teacher. The laws were the laws, weren't they?

"The laws are the laws," her mother admitted. "The problem is sometimes with the pupil." Sadly, she recalled how she had learned these laws and how she had never realized the importance of having a *mikvah* attendant present upon immersion. So, for two long years Mrs. Rabinowitz had immersed without an attendant present. The trouble with this was that as Mrs Rabinowitz didn't like the water, she had only immersed up to her chin. What heartache she had when she discovered she had not fulfilled her obligation to immerse and had remained a *niddah* for all that time.

Suggested List of Items to Bring to the *Mikvah*

(Note: Many *mikvaot* supply some of these items, so verify the necessity to bring your own.)

- [ ] back brush
- [ ] *bedikah* cloths
- [ ] clean pair of colored underwear
- [ ] comb
- [ ] dental floss or toothpicks
- [ ] hair brush
- [ ] handkerchief or tissues
- [ ] makeup remover
- [ ] money (for *mikvah* fee and telephones)
- [ ] nail brush
- [ ] nail filer
- [ ] nail polish remover
- [ ] pumice stone
- [ ] Q-tips
- [ ] rubber slippers
- [ ] scissors
- [ ] scrubbing sponge
- [ ] shampoo
- [ ] small mirror
- [ ] soap
- [ ] toothbrush
- [ ] toothpaste
- [ ] towel

Checklist of Preparations before Immersion

☐ remove any body hair that is generally removed (ideally not on the day of immersion)

☐ cut and file nails

☐ remove nail polish

☐ remove makeup

☐ clean ears and earring holes

☐ clean eyes, eyebrows, lashes

☐ blow and clean nose

☐ wash hair

☐ clean teeth; use toothpick/floss

☐ clean breast nipples

☐ clean navel

☐ wash entire body—pay attention to elbows, knees, spaces between fingers and toes, and the back

☐ smooth hard skin

☐ wash genital areas, also internally

☐ comb all hair

☐ check entire body

☐ use bathroom

☐ remove all jewelry, glasses, lenses, false teeth

CHAPTER 10

A Little Mathematics

**Hilchot Onot: Precautions to Be Taken on the Days
When Anticipating a Period**

THE LAWS OF *Taharat HaMishpachah* enhance a woman's
understanding and appreciation of her physical nature. The
laws of *onot*—meaning the day or night when a woman
anticipates her period—are one of the means by which a
woman gains such self-awareness. These laws require that
she take the proper precautions in order to avoid marital
relations at the expected time of her period lest she begin to
menstruate in the midst of relations and, thus, violate the
severe prohibition against relations at such a time.

Most women's bodies are not clocks, and menstruation
does not begin at an exact predetermined hour. Nevertheless, there are certain patterns which one can observe. The

following laws provide women with guidelines in recognizing those patterns and defining and calculating their *onot*.

The laws of *Taharat HaMishpachah* obligate every Jewish woman to calculate her *onot*. They are designed so that everyone can calculate them on her own. Even those women who shy away from numbers and calculations should not be apprehensive about figuring out the *onot*. One solution for those who are apprehensive is to calculate these times together with their husbands. After all, two heads are better than one. In cases of difficulty, do not hesitate to consult a Rav. Be assured, however, that for many generations, women who never graduated high school and did not possess a college degree in mathematics have been able to calculate their *onot* with ease.

The following definitions are necessary in order to understand these laws:

Onah: the day or night that a woman can be expected to begin her menstruation.

Day: the time from sunrise to sunset.

Night: the time from sunset to sunrise.

The above applies in both the summer (when the days are longer) and the winter (when days are shorter).

Vesset: the menstrual period.

To observe the laws of *onot*, every woman must keep a personal account of the Hebrew calendar date, the exact time, and any specific signs accompanying the onset of her period. The use of a Hebrew calendar is essential for these calculations. There is no way these laws can be kept without it.

An example of the Hebrew calendar date (which is cal-
culated from sunset to sunset):

Tammuz	July
11	Wednesday 8
12	Thursday 9

Sunset this day is 6:50 p.m. If a woman began to menstruate on Wednesday, July 8th, at 4:00 p.m., the Hebrew
date would be the 11th of Tammuz. If she got her period on
Wednesday, July 8th, at 7:00 p.m., the Hebrew date would
be the 12th of Tammuz, accurately called *ohr l'yud bet
Tammuz* and meaning the beginning of the 12th of Tammuz.

It is important to know that the *onah* is determined by
the time of the day, in addition to the date on which a
woman began to menstruate. If menstruation began by day,
her *onah* is during the daytime. If menstruation began at
night, her *onah* is during the night.

The following precautions must be taken at the time of
the *onah*:

1. Marital relations during the *onah* are forbidden. It is
preferable not to hug, kiss, or sleep in the same bed. All
other forms of interaction are permissible.

2. A *bedikah*, the same as performed during the seven
spotless days, is compulsory on the *onah*. If a woman's *onah*
is during the day, it is preferable to do two *bedikot* that day,
one in the morning and one before sunset. If a woman's *onah*
is at night, she should do one *bedikah* at night and one upon
rising in the morning. If a woman's *onah* passes without the
onset of menstruation, and she forgets to carry out the
bedikah, she should, nevertheless, perform one as soon as

she remembers. She is forbidden to have marital relations until she performs a *bedikah*.

3. It is preferable to shower rather than bathe during the *onah*, but if bathing is desired, the required *bedikah* should be carried out beforehand.

Calculating *Onot*

The calculation of *onot* is based on the nature of a woman's menstrual cycle. There are two categories of cycles: the regular and the irregular.

1. The regular cycle: Termed in Hebrew the *vesset kavua*, it is established when it occurs for three successive months at a fixed time as defined by the halacha. A woman is said to have a regular cycle when the onset of menstruation occurs on three consecutive occasions during the same *onah*, either on the same Hebrew date, *vesset hachodesh*, or after three identical intervals, *vesset haflagah*. Conversely, a *vesset kavua* is nullified when, for three successive months, menstruation does not begin on the expected date. A Rav *must* be consulted to verify the establishment (or cancellation) of this type of cycle, for the laws are extremely detailed. In fact, there are thirteen types of halachically defined regularities.

Important note: Nowadays, the regular cycle is quite a rare phenomenon.

(There are other types of *vesstot kavuot*, one called *vesset haguf*, when menstruation is expected because of specific physical symptoms, and one called *vesset al yidei maaseh*, when menstruation is associated with a particular activity. These *vesstot* can be established without any connection to the occurrence of menstruation on a specific *onah*. At times, however, the two concepts are combined, and a woman's *vesset* is established according to both a fixed time and a fixed physical symptom.)

2.   The irregular cycle: This is termed in Hebrew *vesset lo kavua*. The menstrual cycles of most women today are governed by the rules associated with this *vesset*. Even if a woman gets her period at approximately the same time monthly, she must nevertheless, because of her irregularity, observe the following guidelines to determine her *onot*. On these days, she must follow the precautions involving separation and *bedikot* described above.

Note: Many of the *onot* often fall on the same day. Thus, actually, one ends up taking the required precautions for only a few days each month.

Important: All calculations are from the first day of the last period.

Remember: All calculations are according to the Hebrew calendar date which is from sunset to sunset.

Onot on Which the Precautions Are Required for a Woman with an Irregular Cycle

1.   *Onat hachodesh*—monthly *onah*: the Hebrew calendar date on which menstruation began the previous month. This *onah* will be either at night or during the day, depending on the time of the onset of her last period.

Example: A woman's previous menstrual period began on the 13th of Tishrei by day. Her *onah* will be on the 13th of Cheshvan during the daytime.

2.   *Onat haflagah*—the interval *onah*: the number of days between her last two menstrual periods. In calculating this

interval a woman counts from the first day of her second to last period to the first day of her last period *including in this count the first days of both periods* (e.g., the interval between Sunday and Friday is six days). This *onah*, too, will either be during the day or at night, depending on when her last period began.

Example: A woman's second to last period began on the 1st of Tammuz at night. Her last period occurred on the 3rd of Av by day. The interval between them is thirty-two days. Her *onah* will be on the 4th of Elul during the daytime— thirty-two days after the 3rd of Av.

(Some authorities recommend the adoption of an additional stringency regarding *onat hachodesh* and *onat haflagah* and suggest that the precautions required for the *onah* also be observed during the previous day or night.)

3.   *Onah beinonit*—the common *onah*: the 30th day from a woman's last menstrual period. According to many authorities, it is preferable to regard the 31st day also as the *onah beinonit* and observe the precautions then, as well. This *onah* lasts twenty-four hours for each day (forty-eight hours when observing both the 30th and 31st days) and is one night and day on the Hebrew calendar.

Example: A woman's last period began on the 23rd of Shevat. The 30th day is the night and day of the 22nd of Adar (and the 31st day is the night and day of the 23rd of Adar).*

---

*Hebrew months always have either twenty-nine or thirty days. Whenever a Hebrew month has twenty-nine days, the 30th day, (observed as the *onah beinonit* by all) and the *onat hachodesh* will be the same. Whenever a Hebrew month has thirty days, the 31st day (when observed as the *onah beinonit*) and the *onat hachodesh* will be the same.

(Some authorities hold that a woman who *never* menstruates until after the 30th day is not obligated to keep the precautions of the *onah beinonit*.)

An additional rule applies to a woman whose period always begins after an interval differing by no more than three days. For example, if she always begins menstruating between the 26th and 29th day of her menstrual cycle, then, in addition to keeping the above *onot*, she must check herself before and after intercourse on any one of these days which is not her *onah* that month.

4. *Vesset haguf*—menstruation that begins immediately after the appearance of bodily symptoms: A woman who always experiences *specific physical symptoms* immediately prior to the onset of her period must consider herself as likely to menstruate and must observe the precautions described above. (This does not refer to the general feelings of headache, cramps, nausea, and the like which commonly precede the onset of a woman's period.) This type of phenomenon is quite rare, and requires consultation with a Rav to determine its nature.

Laws of *Onot* Applying to Women Who Are *Misulakot Damim*— Those Who Do Not Usually Menstruate

The Rabbis have determined three situations which place women in this category:

1. Pregnancy: Women who generally do not menstruate during pregnancy are not required to observe *onot*. A woman who does menstruate during pregnancy must observe the *onot* according to the laws of a woman with an irregular

cycle. This applies even if she has a regular cycle and menstruates on those days.

If a woman does not menstruate, the following laws apply: A woman with an irregular cycle must observe the precautions in the first month of pregnancy. After that time, since she is no longer menstruating, there is no need for further strictures. A woman with a regular cycle must observe the precautions on the appropriate day for the first three months. (A woman with a regular cycle of *onat haflagah* does not need to take precautions after the first month.)

2.   Childbirth: A woman who gives birth (or miscarries) need not observe the *onah* precautions during the first twenty-four months after giving birth unless she menstruates. Should she menstruate within these twenty-four months, she must observe the *onah* precautions of a woman with an irregular cycle.

(If a woman had a regular cycle before giving birth, according to the halacha, she need not take the precautions appropriate to her regular cycle until after twenty-four months. Nowadays, however, it is customary for her to observe these precautions during these twenty-four months if she resumes menstruating.)

3.   Menopause: A woman who did not have a regular cycle before menopause need not take any *onah* precautions once she stops menstruating. Should she menstruate again, she must take the same precautions as for an irregular cycle.

It is customary for a woman who had a regular cycle before menopause to continue taking her usual *onah* precautions until the menses do not occur for six months. If she menstruates after this point, she follows the *onah* precautions observed by women with an irregular cycle.

A Sample Calendar

A. A woman got her period Saturday, the 1st of Nissan, March 19, at 4:00 p.m. [Sunset is at 6:00 p.m.] Thus, her *onah* is by *day*.

Onot for Iyar are as follows:

B. *Onah Beinonit* — Common *Onah*. 30th day = 30th of Nissan, Sunday, April 17. *Onah* extends from sunset Saturday until sunset Sunday.

C. 31st day = 1st of Iyar, Monday, April 18. *Onah* extends from sunset Sunday until sunset Monday.

D. *Onat Hachodesh* — Monthly *Onah*. 1st of Iyar, Monday, April 18. *Onah* extends from sunrise until sunset.

Month of Iyar

E. The woman's next period began on MONDAY NIGHT, April 18, at 7:00 PM which is the beginning of Tuesday, the 2nd of Iyar. (Sunset is at 6:20 P.M. Thus, *onah* is at night.

Onot for Sivan are as follows:

F. *Onah Beinonit* — Common *Onah*. 30th day = 2nd of Sivan, Wednesday, May 18. *Onah* extends from sunset Tuesday until sunset Wednesday.

G. 31st day = 3rd of Sivan, Thursday, May 19. *Onah* extends from sunset Wednesday until sunset Thursday.

H. *Onat Hachodesh* — Monthly *Onah*. 2nd of Sivan, Wednesday, May 18. *Onah* extends from sunset Tuesday, until sunrise Wednesday.

I. *Onat Haflagah* — Interval *Onah*. Interval between periods is thirty-two days. 4th of Sivan, Friday, May 20th. *Onah* extends from sunset Thursday until sunrise Friday.

Hebrew calendar dates are in **bold**

Month of March — Adar/Nissan

Sun	Mon	Tue	Wed	Thu	Fri	Sat
			1	**2**	**3**	**4**	**5**
6	**7**	**8**	**9**	**10**	**11**	**12**
13	**14**	**15**	**16**	**17**	**18**	**1**[A] **19**
2 **20**	3 **21**	4 **22**	5 **23**	6 **24**	7 **25**	8 **26**
9 **27**	10 **28**	11 **29**	12 **30**	13 **31**		

Month of April — Nissan/Iyar

Sun	Mon	Tue	Wed	Thu	Fri	Sat
					14 1	**15** 2
16 3	**17** 4	**18** 5	**19** 6	**20** 7	**21** 8	**22** 9
23 10	**24** 11	**25** 12	**26** 13	**27** 14	**28** 15	**29** 16
30 17	**1**[B] 18	**2**[C] 19	**3**[D] 20	**4**[E] 21	**5** 22	**6** 23
7 24	**8** 25	**9** 26	**10** 27	**11** 28	**12** 29	**13** 30

Month of May — Iyar/Sivan

Sun	Mon	Tue	Wed	Thu	Fri	Sat
14 1	**15** 2	**16** 3	**17** 4	**18** 5	**19** 6	**20** 7
21 8	**22** 9	**23** 10	**24** 11	**25** 12	**26** 13	**27** 14
28 15	**29** 16	**1** 17[F]	**2** 18[H]	**3** 19[G]	**4** 20	**5** 21[I]
6 22	**7** 23	**8** 24	**9** 25	**10** 26	**11** 27	**12** 28
13 29	**14** 30	**15** 31				

CHAPTER 11

Brides and Grooms

EVERY MARRIAGE IS considered a microcosm of the ultimate wedding relationship, the bond between God and the Jewish People, and every Jewish home is considered a miniature sanctuary. Thus, the couple's marriage day represents the day on which the *Shechinah*, the Divine Presence, descends to rest between them.

Accordingly, the day of a couple's wedding should be marked by appropriate behavior. In contrast to the reckless frivolity which sometimes precedes secular marriages, Jewish tradition views the wedding day as one of holiness and sanctity. Indeed, our Sages describe it as a personal "Yom Kippur" for the bride and groom. All their sins are forgiven, and they are given exceptional spiritual energies with which to face the new challenges married life will bring.

The wedding day should be set aside for *teshuvah*—repentance, *tefillah*—prayer, and *tzedakah*—charity. It is customary for both the bride and groom to fast on their wedding day. (If either fear that fasting will be too difficult, a Rav should be consulted.) The confessional prayers recited on *erev* Yom Kippur are said, and it customary to ask one's parents for forgiveness. Moreover, the bride and groom should give generously to charity on their wedding day. Our Sages relate that in the midst of the busy preparations of her wedding day, Rabbi Akiva's daughter took time out to give a meal to a hungry wayfarer. The next morning a poisonous snake was found by her bed, pierced by her hair clip. Without knowing it, she had killed the snake when she took down her hair. We are told that it was in the merit of her generosity that she was saved.

Laws Regarding a Wedding

1. Every bride should consult a Rav or her *Taharat Ha-Mishpachah* counselor to assist her in determining the date for her wedding.

2. As close as possible to the wedding date, every bride must make a *hefsek taharah* and count seven spotless days. She then immerses in a *mikvah*.

3. Most preferably, the immersion should be on the night before the wedding. In any case, the immersion should not take place more than four days before the wedding.

4. A bride may immerse on the eighth day, during the day, after the seven spotless days. (If the wedding coincides with

the seventh day of the seven spotless days, a Rav should be consulted as to the time of immersion.)

5.   It is the Ashkenazic custom to do a *bedikah* every day until, and including, the wedding day.*

6.   After intercourse has taken place, a virgin bride is considered a *niddah* whether she discovers hymenal bleeding or not. (If there is a doubt whether complete intercourse has taken place, consult a Rav. This must be determined on an individual basis. Painful sensations or the presence of blood are factors taken into consideration.)

7.   After intercourse has taken place, a virgin bride need only wait *four* days before making a *hefsek taharah* and counting seven spotless days prior to immersing in a *mikvah*. If she menstruates in the meantime, she must wait the minimum *five* days, as usual, before the *hefsek taharah* and seven spotless days.

8.   Upon marriage, a woman must verify that intercourse does not induce menstruation. She does this by performing a *bedikah*, prior to and following intercourse, at the first three opportunities she has after hymenal bleeding has ceased and on her "unsafe" days.

   (Most women who do not have a regular cycle nevertheless have a fixed number of days before which they never expect their period. For example: a woman does not get her period before the 25th day of her cycle, but after the 25th, she could get her period at any time. The days from her immersion until the 25th are considered her "safe days,"

---

*The Ashkenazic custom is that the bride and groom refrain from seeing each other prior to the wedding from the time she does the *hefsek taharah*. The Sephardic custom places no restriction on the bride and groom seeing each other, even on the day of the wedding.

while the days after the 25th are called her "unsafe" days.)

During her safe days she is compared to a woman with a regular cycle who is not obligated to check herself before and after intercourse. Only after these safe days have passed should a woman with an irregular cycle do the three *bedikot*. (Her husband should also check himself for blood after intercourse at these times.)

After completing this process of verification three times, the couple need not check themselves further. They may rest assured that intercourse will not cause the woman to menstruate.

A woman who sights blood after intercourse (after her hymenal bleeding has totally ceased), should consult a doctor and a Rav. If this occurs once after intercourse, she should check herself the next time after intercourse.

Chupat Niddah—A Wedding Conducted While the Bride is a *Niddah*

When a bride is a *niddah* at her wedding, the couple may not engage in any intimacy. Slightly different practices must be carried out at the wedding, and the newlywed couple are forbidden to spend the night alone until the bride has immersed. There are various options available under these circumstances, and a Rav should be consulted to determine the best solution for each couple.

The occurrence of a *chupat niddah* is obviously something every bride and groom tries to avoid. The bride should keep a personal calendar before marriage and consult it in planning the date of her wedding.

(There is absolutely no obligation to try to avoid a *chupat niddah* by taking birth control pills. This practice may be permitted, but is definitely not encouraged. If she is considering taking the pill, a bride should discuss the matter seriously with a Rav, a doctor, and her future husband. Pills may only be taken in a case of a definite *chupat niddah* and not when it is only in doubt. It must be emphasized that such a step can backfire, as these pills sometimes cause spotting.)

Often, not everything works out as we plan. If a *chupat niddah* occurs (despite a couple's efforts), they should remember that everything is predestined. Thousands of other couples have faced this challenge, and, as our Sages teach, "God does not come to His creations with overburdening demands" (*Avodah Zarah* 3a). Whenever God presents man with a challenge, He provides him with the inner strength to overcome it. This awkward situation lasts only a few days. Afterward, a couple can enjoy a lifetime of marital joy.

CHAPTER 12

Childbirth and Childbearing

1. A WOMAN IN labor, prior to actual childbirth, is considered a *niddah* from the moment her contractions are so intense they incapacitate her (i.e., she cannot walk around anymore and needs to lie down).

2. The show of blood which often precipitates the onset of labor renders a woman a *niddah*.

3. The breaking of the bag of waters does not necessarily render a woman a *niddah*. For determination, a Rav should be consulted.

4. Childbirth renders a woman a *niddah*.

5. Once a woman enters the *niddah* state for any of the above reasons, all the *harchakot* that are generally observed must be followed. Thus, her husband may not

look at the parts of her body that are usually covered, and he may not touch her or hand objects directly to her.

6. According to the halacha, a woman may immerse in the *mikvah* on completion of seven days after the birth of a son and on completion of fourteen days after the birth of a daughter—provided she has made a *hefsek taharah* and counted seven spotless days.

Practically, most women find that they cannot successfully perform a *hefsek taharah* until at least six to eight weeks after childbirth. (This coincides with most medical advice which suggests that a woman wait until her postnatal checkup—six weeks after childbirth—to resume marital relations.) If three months have passed, and a woman is still unable to achieve seven spotless days, she should consult a doctor and a Rav.

7. In case of a miscarriage, a woman may immerse in the *mikvah* on completion of seven days if the sex of the fetus could be determined as male. If its sex was female or could not be determined, the completion of fourteen days is required. Needless to say, the above only applies provided the woman has performed a *hefsek taharah* and has counted seven spotless days.

Concerning Birth Control

Rabbi Cohen was invited to lecture at a women's convention. At one of the sessions, the topic concerned the pursuit of a career outside the home. The Rabbi kept the audience spellbound, elaborating on the fulfillment, joy, growth, and satisfaction a woman can find within her own home. He did not rule out the possibility of an outside career, but only provided the woman has her priorities in the right order and recognizes her responsibilities at home.

One woman in the audience found Rabbi Cohen's ideas difficult to accept. She had been trained to look at motherhood as a burdensome yoke and a career as a woman's chance for "liberation." "Rabbi," she said, requesting the floor, "pardon me for being so rude and nosy, but what does *your* wife do?"

"*My* wife?" the Rabbi exclaimed, "Why, she runs a children's shelter for eight children. She tends to their physical, emotional, and psychological needs. She monitors their growth, enriches their learning experiences, and encourages their appreciation for culture and the arts. She plays the role of teacher, nurse, chauffeur, companion, and cook, among others, and it's all done with devotion and joy!"

The audience applauded with approval. Here was a truly liberated woman, dedicating her abilities and skills to benefit unfortunate children.

"By the way," concluded Rabbi Cohen with a smile, "Those eight children are our own...."

The women could not help but grin sheepishly. They recognized the absurdity of social standards that would consider the Rabbi's wife's occupation as a respectable career provided it was someone else's children she was raising, but not her own!

In contrast, the Torah regards motherhood and home-keeping with the utmost respect. A woman is encouraged to enjoy the blessing of children and not to view the process of raising them as a burden or barrier to her own personal growth.

The very first mitzvah in the Torah is "Be fruitful and multiply" (*Bereshit* 1:28). God grants every woman precisely the number of children she is fit to handle. If she dedicates herself to the role of motherhood, this will be positively reflected in her children, grandchildren, and in their offspring for many generations to come.

The Torah considers the presence of children as the very source of blessing in the home. "A man should wish for and desire offspring, beseeching God to grant him a household of sons and daughters. He should then guide and raise them to serve God" *(Sefer Hakedushah)*.

The Torah describes a natural, divine plan for child spacing that works in accordance with a woman's physical makeup. Thus, a breast-feeding woman is referred to by the halacha as *mesuleket damim*, infertile, which she usually was for as long as two years after childbirth. Even today, when physical nature has changed, many women who breast-feed exclusively find that they often cannot conceive during this time. However, even a woman who becomes fertile during that time should look upon the possibility for bringing children into the world as a divine blessing.

Laws Concerning Birth Control

1. Birth control is not permitted unless a Rav is consulted and he specifically rules that a couple may use contraception. A husband and wife cannot rely upon a decision given to another couple.

2. One may not postpone the proper time for *mikvah* immersion for this purpose unless permitted to do so by a Rav.

3. A woman who has a physiological, psychological, or emotional need to practice birth control, should, together with her husband, consult a Rav. Only he is given Torah authority to decide when birth control may be practiced, for how long, and by which method.

In order for the Rav to assist her, a woman should present all medical information to him. In addition, she should be sure to state her feelings and needs. Thus, the Rav will be in a position to render a decision and guide her sensitively. Each situation must be viewed individually within the context of Torah law. This is because the Torah stresses that one must "live by them [the *mitzvot*]" (*VaYikra* 18:5)— and not live in misery. What may be acceptable for one couple may not be suitable for another.

One should constantly bear in mind that the all-encompassing task of raising children is acknowledged by thousands of families as the height of joy and fulfillment with no comparison to any other type of satisfaction. Raising children can certainly be considered a "profession" and a mother surely worthy of the title "professional."

The difficulties and challenges entailed in this noteworthy profession should be viewed in light of the words of our Sages: "The reward comes in relation to the difficulties" (*Avot* 5:23). In addition to the *nachas* and pleasure derived in this world, a woman's ultimate reward is a position of honor in the world to come.

Index to *Halachot*

Becoming a *Niddah*

Hefsek Taharah and *Shiva Niki'im*

Jewish Marriage Education

Established with the Encouragement and Guidance of
HAGAON HARAV **SHLOMO ZALMAN AUERBACH** Zt"l

In Consultation with
HAGAON HARAV **YOSEF SHOLOM ELYASHIV** Shlita
Halachic Consultant
HARAV **YISROEL GANS** Shlita

Women seeking Taharat Hamishpachah counsellors or women wishing to train as teachers in any country may obtain further information from the International Office of Jewish Marriage Education:

J.M.E. International
POB 43206
Jerusalem, 91400 Israel
Tel/Fax: 972-8-974-1030

JME North America
6 Gel Court
Monsey, NY 10952 USA
Tel: 1-914-426-6678
Fax: 1-914-426-2268

JME Europe
64 Whitehall Road
Gateshead, NE8 4ET England
Tel/Fax: 44-191-477-0620

JME South America
Rua Peixoto Gomide 2,054/5
CEP 01409-002 SP
Sao Paulo, Brazil
Tel/Fax: 55-11-3064-4850

JME South Africa
195 Frances St., Observatory
Johannesburg 2198
Tel/Fax: 27-11-648-5583

This book is also available in Hebrew, Yiddish, Russian, French, Spanish, Portugese, and Braille. For information on obtaining copies, please contact one of the above addresses.